HAVE YOU H
THE
SUN SINGI

GW00734326

HAVE YOU HEARD THE SUN SINGING?

Poems collected by Adrian Rumble

Bell & Hyman

For Mary, Joanna, Corinna and Kristian.
And in memory of my father and my brother.

Published by
Bell & Hyman Limited
an imprint of Unwin Hyman Limited
Denmark House
37–39 Queen Elizabeth Street
London SE1 2QB

First published in 1981 by Evans Brothers Limited
This anthology © 1983 Bell & Hyman Limited
Illustrations © 1983 Bell & Hyman Limited
Reprinted 1987
Cover and illustrations by Mary Budd

British Library Cataloguing in Publication Data
Have you heard the sun singing?
    I Rumble, Adrian
    821'.9'1408

ISBN 0 7135 1456 6

Printed in Great Britain by Biddles Ltd.,
Guildford and King's Lynn

Contents

Tubs of Thunder, Fists of Rain
The weather and seasons

Gold for a Princess's Crown
The senses, colours, words, the beauty of machines

Main Deep
Sea and seashore; tales of the ocean

What if the Hills should Stir?
Familiar things in a new light, strange fancies

Green Man, Blue Man
Magic, witches, mystery and monsters

I Dreamt I Caught a Little Owl
Night-time, dreams, night fears, space

My Mother Saw a Dancing Bear
Animals, both wild and domestic

Loaves of Blue Heaven
Birds

Marbles in My Pocket
Games, school, tongue twisters

TUBS OF THUNDER
FISTS OF RAIN

Go Out

Eileen Mathias

Go out
When the wind's about;
Let him buffet you
Inside out.

Go out
In a rainy drizzle;
Never sit by the fire
To sizzle.

Go out
When the snowflakes play;
Toss them about
On the white highway.

Go out
And stay till night;
When the sun is shedding
Its golden light.

River Winding

Charlotte Zolotow

Rain falling, what things do you grow?
Snow melting, where do you go?
Wind blowing, what trees do you know?
River winding, where do you flow?

Have you Heard the Sun Singing?

From Jazz for five

John Smith

Have you ever heard the sun in the sky
Man have you heard it?
Have you heard it break the black of night
Man have you heard it?
Have you heard it shouting its songs, have you heard
It scorch up the air like a phoenix bird,
Have you heard the sun singing?

It ain't gonna rain no more, no more

Anon

It ain't gonna rain no more, no more,
It ain't gonna rain no more;
How in the heck can I wash my neck
If it ain't gonna rain no more?

Clouds

Anon

Mackerel sky,
Mackerel sky,
Not long wet,
And not long dry.

Rainy nights

Irene Thompson

I like the town on rainy nights
  When everything is wet –
When all the town has magic lights
  And streets of shining jet!

When all the rain about the town
  Is like a looking-glass,
And all the lights are upside down
  Below me as I pass.

In all the pools are velvet skies,
  And down the dazzling street
A fairy city gleams and lies
  In beauty at my feet.

Didn't it rain

Anon

Now, didn't it rain, chillun,
God's gonna 'stroy this world with water,
Now didn't it rain, my Lord,
Now didn't it rain, rain, rain.

Well, it rained forty days and it rained forty nights,
There wasn't no land nowhere in sight,
God sent a raven to carry the news,
He histe his wings and away he flew

Well, it rained forty days and forty nights without stopping,
Noah was glad when the rain stopped a-dropping.
God sent Noah a rainbow sign,
Says, "No more water, but fire next time."

They knocked at the window and they knocked at the
                door.
They cried, "O Noah, please take me on board."
Noah cried, "You're full of sin,
The Lord's got the key and you can't get in."

Wellingtons

Daphne Lister

Wellies, wellies, wellingtons,
Wellingtons are fun,
Wear them on a rainy day
And no harm can be done.

Splish and splash and splosh and splush
Through puddles and the gutter,
Wellies keep your feet quite dry,
So mother will not mutter.

Socks will not be wringing wet,
So there should be no sneezes,
You don't catch cold with wellies on,
Or get bad coughs and wheezes.

Splish and Splash and Splosh and Splush,
Until you see the sun,
Raw and rotten rainy days
With wellies on are fun!

Rain

Elizabeth Jennings

Beautiful rain
Falling so softly
Such a delicate thing

The harvests need you
And some of the flowers
But we too

Because you remind
Of coolness of quiet
Of tenderest words

Come down rain, fall
Not too harshly but give
Your strange sense of peace to us.

Who has seen the wind?

Christina Rossetti

Who has seen the wind?
  Neither I nor you:
But when the leaves hang trembling
  The wind is passing through.

Who has seen the wind?
  Neither you nor I:
But when the trees bow down their heads
  The wind is passing by.

Praise Song of the Wind

Traditional
Siberian translation by W Radloff and Willard R Trask

Trees with weak roots
I will strike, I the wind.
I will roar, I will whistle.

Haycocks built today
I will scatter, I the wind.
I will roar, I will whistle.

Badly made haycocks
I will carry off, I the wind.
I will roar, I will whistle.

Uncovered stacks of sheaves
I will soak through, I the wind.
I will roar, I will whistle.

Houses not tightly roofed
I will destroy, I the wind.
I will roar, I will whistle.

Hay piled in sheds
I will tear apart, I the wind.
I will roar, I will whistle.

Fire kindled in the road
I will set flickering, I the wind.
I will roar, I will whistle.

Houses with bad smoke-holes
I will shake, I the wind.
I will roar, I will whistle.

The farmer who does not think
I will make to think, I the wind.
I will roar, I will whistle.

The worthless slug-a-bed
I will wake, I the wind.
I will roar, I will whistle.

The Wind

N Carey (II)

The wind,
It is a ghostly hand
Pushing to and fro
The leaves and stray paper
That lie scattered in his path.

The trees
Bow down to the strength
Of the whistling wind,
As though paying homage
To some unknown king.

The Wind

James Stephens

The wind stood up and gave a shout;
He whistled on his fingers, and

Kicked the withered leaves about,
And thumped the branches with his hand.

And said he'll kill, and kill, and kill;
And so he will! And so he will!

The Wind

James Reeves

I can get through a doorway without any key,
And strip the leaves from the great oak tree.
I can drive storm-clouds and shake tall towers,
Or steal through a garden and not wake the flowers.
Seas I can move and ships I can sink;
I can carry a house-top or the scent of a pink.
When I am angry I can rave and riot;
And when I am spent, I lie quiet as quiet.

Windy Nights

Rodney Bennett

Rumbling in the chimneys,
   Rattling at the doors,
Round the roofs and round the roads
  The rude wind roars;
Raging through the darkness,
   Raving through the trees,
Racing off again across
   The great grey seas.

Rain

Shel Silverstein

I opened my eyes
And looked up at the rain
And it dripped in my head
And flowed into my brain
So pardon this wild crazy thing I just said
I'm just not the same since there's rain in my head.
I step very softly
I walk very slow
I can't do a hand-stand
Or I might overflow.
And all I can hear as I lie in my bed
Is the slishity-slosh of the rain in my head.

From the Fog

Charles Reznikoff

From the fog a gull flies slowly
and is lost in fog. The buildings are only clouds.

The Fog

W H Davies

I saw the fog grow thick,
  Which soon made blind my ken;
It made tall men of boys,
  And giants of tall men.

It clutched my throat, I coughed;
  Nothing was in my head
Except two heavy eyes
  Like balls of burning lead.

And when it grew so black
  That I could know no place,
I lost all judgement then,
  Of distance and of space.

The street lamps, and the lights
  Upon the halted cars,
Could either be on earth
  Or be the heavenly stars.

A man passed by me close,
  I asked my way, he said,
"Come, follow me, my friend" -
  I followed where he led.

He rapped the stones in front,
  "Trust me", he said, "and come":
I followed like a child —
  ˄ blind man led me home.

Fog

Carl Sandburg

The fog comes
on little cat feet.

It sits looking
over harbour and city
on silent haunches
and then moves on.

The Fog

F R McCreary

Slowly, the fog,
Hunch-shouldered with a grey face,
Arms wide, advances,
Finger tips touching the way
Past the dark houses
And dark gardens of roses.
Up the short street from the harbour,
Slowly the fog,
Seeking, seeking;
Arms wide, shoulders hunched,
Searching, searching.
Out through the streets to the fields,
Slowly, the fog –
A blind man hunting the moon.

Thunder and Lightning

James Kirkup

Blood punches through every vein
As lightning strips the windowpane.

Under its flashing whip, a white
Village leaps to light.

On tubs of thunder, fists of rain
Slog it out of sight again.

Blood punches the heart with fright
As rain belts the village night.

Change

Charlotte Zolotow

The summer
still hangs
heavy and sweet
with sunlight
as it did last year.

The autumn
still comes
showering gold and crimson
as it did last year.

The winter
still stings
clean and cold and white
as it did last year.

The spring
still comes
like a whisper in the dark night.

It is only I
who have changed.

in Just—

e e cummings

in Just—
spring   when the world is mud—
luscious the little
lame balloonman

whistles   far   and wee

and eddieandbill come
running from marbles and
piracies and it's
spring

when the world is puddle-wonderful

the queer
old balloonman whistles
far   and   wee
and bettyandisbel come dancing

from hop-scotch and jump-rope and

it's
spring
and
    the

        goat-footed

balloonMan whistles
far
and
wee

The Spring Wind

Charlotte Zolotow

The summer wind
is soft and sweet
the winter wind is strong
the autumn wind is mischievous
and sweeps the leaves along.

The wind I love the best
comes gently after rain
smelling of spring and growing things
brushing the world with feathery wings
while everything glistens, and everything sings
in the spring wind
after the rain.

Leaves and Fires

Leonard Clark

They are raking the leaves in the parks of the town,
They are dying, the leaves, they are all falling down,
Twirling and whirling, the leaves die away,
Falling all night, raking all day.

They are stoking the fires in the parks of the town,
They are smoking, the fires, they are all burning brown,
Sweeping and piling, the fires are alight,
Burning all day, smoking all night.

For Autumn

Eleanor Farjeon

O my sweet Nightingales, why are you dumb again?
O my blue Violets, when will you come again?
O my brown Bees in the yellow Lime-Trees,
Humble-Bees, Bumble-Bees, when will you hum again?

Autumn Fires

Robert Louis Stevenson

In the other gardens
   And all up the vale,
From the autumn bonfires
   See the smoke trail!

Pleasant summer over
   And all the summer flowers,
The red fire blazes,
   The grey smoke towers.

Sing a song of seasons!
   Something bright in all!
Flowers in the summer,
   Fires in the Fall!

From The One Singer

W H Davies

Dead leaves from off the tree
Make whirlpools on the ground;
Like dogs that chase their tails,
Those leaves go round and round;
Like birds unfledged and young,
The old bare branches cry;
Branches that shake and bend
To feel the winds go by.

From November Night

Adelaide Crapsey

Listen . . .
With faint dry sound,
Like steps of passing ghosts,
The leaves, frost-crisped, break from the trees
And fall.

From Gathering Leaves

Robert Frost

Spades take up leaves
No better than spoons,
And bags full of leaves
Are light as balloons.

I make a great noise
Of rustling all day
Like rabbit and deer
Running away.

But the mountains I raise
Elude my embrace,
Flowing over my arms
And into my face.

Something told the wild geese

Rachel Field

Something told the wild geese
   It was time to go,
Though the fields lay golden
   Something whispered, 'Snow!'
Leaves were green and stirring,
   Berries, luster-glossed,
But beneath warm feathers
   Something cautioned, 'Frost!'

All the sagging orchards
   Steamed with amber spice,
But each wild breast stiffened
   At remembered ice.
Something told the wild geese
   It was time to fly –
Summer sun was on their wings,
   Winter in their cry.

An Autumn Morning

Anon

It seems like a dream
   In the garden today;
The trees, once so green,
   With rich colours are gay.

The oak is aglow
   With a warm, crimson blush;
The maple leaves show
   A deep purple flush.

The elm tree with bold
   Yellow patches is bright,
And with pale gleaming gold
   The beech seems alight.

And the creeper leaves flare
   Like red flame on the wall;
Their dazzle and glare
   Is the brightest of all.

The big chestnut trees
   Are all russet and brown
And everywhere leaves
   One by one flutter down.

And all the leaves seem
   To be dressed up so gay
That it seems like a dream
   In the garden today.

Autumn

T E Hulme

A touch of cold in the autumn night –
I walked abroad,
And saw the ruddy moon lean over a hedge
Like a red faced farmer.
I did not stop to speak, but nodded,
And round about were the wistful stars
With white faces like town children.

In the Wood

Eileen Mathias

Cold winter's in the wood,
   I saw him pass
Crinkling up fallen leaves
   Along the grass.

Bleak winter's in the wood,
   The birds have flown
Leaving the naked trees
   Shivering alone.

King Winter's in the wood,
   I saw him go
Crowned with a coronet
   Of crystal snow.

Haiku

J W Hackett

A bitter morning:
   sparrows sitting together
    without any necks.

Snowing

Olive Dove

Snowing. Snowing. Snowing.
Woolly petals tossed down
From a tremendous tree in the sky
By a giant hand, the hand
That switches on lightning
And tips down cloudbursts.
I like to think of it that way.

Quiet. Quiet. Quiet.
No noise from the traffic in the street.
In the classroom only Miss Nil's voice
Dictating and the rustle of paper.
I am holding my breath in wonder.
I want to cry out 'Look! Look!'
Miss Nil has paused between sentences
And is looking out of the window.
But I suppose she is wondering whether
She'll have to abandon her car and walk home.

Snowing. Snowing. Snowing.
I wish I could go out and taste it.
Feel it nestling against my cheek.
And trickling through my fingers.
The message has come round we are to go home now
Because the buses may stop running.
So the snow has given us a whole hour of freedom.
I pick up fistfuls.
Squeeze them hard and hurl them

But hurry, the bus is coming
And I want to get home early to look at the garden:
At the holly tree in its polar bear coat;
The cherries with white arms upstretched,
Naked of leaves; the scratchy claw marks
Of birds, and blobs of big pawed dogs.
And I want to make footprints of my own
Where the snow is a blank page for scribbling.
Tea time already. Still the snow comes down.
Migrating moths, millions and millions
Dizzying down out of the darkening sky.

Mother draws the curtains.
Why couldn't they stay open?
Now I can't watch the secretive birds
Descending, the stealthy army invading.
What does the roof look like
Covered with slabs of cream?
How high are the heaps on window ledges?
Tomorrow the snow may have begun to melt away.
O, why didn't I look more
While there was still time?

Winter the Huntsman

Osbert Sitwell

Through his iron glades
Rides Winter the Huntsman.
All colour fades
As his horn is heard sighing.

Far through the forest
His wild hooves crash and thunder
Till many a mighty branch
Is torn asunder.

As the red reynard creeps
To his hole near the river,
The copper leaves fall
And the bare trees shiver.

As night creeps from the ground,
Hides each tree from its brother,
And each dying sound
Reveals yet another.

Is it Winter the Huntsman
Who gallops through his iron glades,
Cracking his cruel whip
To the gathering shades?

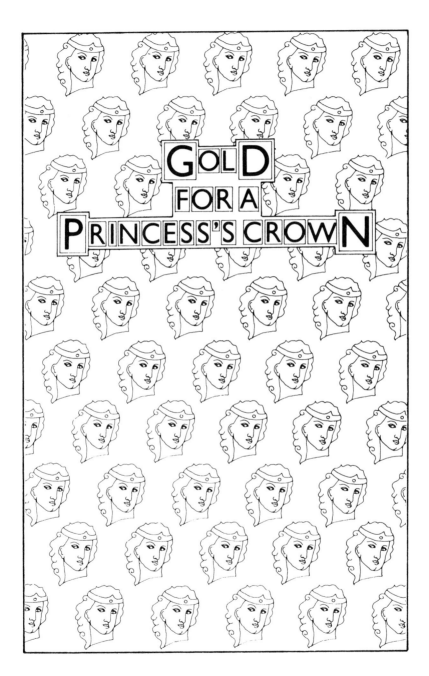

GOLD FOR A PRINCESS'S CROWN

Shining Things

Elizabeth Gould

I love all shining things —
      the lovely moon,
The silver stars at night,
      gold sun at noon.
A glowing rainbow in
      a stormy sky,
Or bright clouds hurrying
      when wind goes by.

I love the glow-worm's elf-light
      in the lane,
And leaves a-shine with glistening
      drops of rain,
The glinting wings of bees,
      and butterflies,
My purring pussy's green
      and shining eyes.

I love the street-lamps shining
      through the gloom;
Tall candles lighted in
      a shadowy room,
New-tumbled chestnuts from
      the chestnut tree,
And gleaming fairy bubbles
      blown by me.

I love the shining buttons
        on my coat,
I love the bright beads round
        my mother's throat.
I love the coppery flames
        of red and gold.
That cheer and comfort me
        when I'm a-cold.

The beauty of all shining things
        is yours and mine,
It was a *lovely* thought of God
        to make things shine.

Look

John Smith

I eat from the dish of the world
    Trees, fields, flowers.
I drink from the glass of space
    Blue sea, sky.

I pour the sky over me
    In blue showers.
Look! I light up the day
    With my eye.

Trees

Sara Coleridge

The Oak is called the King of Trees,
The Aspen quivers in the breeze,
The Poplar grows up straight and tall,
The Pear-tree spreads along the wall,
The Sycamore gives pleasant shade,
The Willow droops in watery glade,
The Fir-tree useful timber gives,
The Beech amid the forest lives.

The Rainbow

Walter de la Mare

I saw the lovely arch
Of Rainbow span the sky,
The gold sun burning
As the rain swept by.

In bright-ringed solitude
The showery foliage shone
One lovely moment,
And the Bow was gone.

The Flint

Christina Rossetti

An emerald is as green as grass:
   A ruby red as blood:
A sapphire shines as blue as heaven;
   But a flint lies in the mud

A diamond is a brilliant stone,
   To catch the world's desire;
An opal holds a rainbow light:
   But a flint holds fire.

Grey

James Reeves

Grey is the sky, and grey the woodman's cot
With grey smoke tumbling from the chimney-pot.
The flagstones are grey that lead to the door;
Grey is the hearth, and grey the worn old floor.

The old man by the fire nods in his chair;
Grey are his clothes and silvery grey his hair.
Grey are the shadows around him creeping,
And grey the mouse from the corner peeping.

Colours

Christina Rossetti

What is pink? A rose is pink
By the fountain's brink.
What is red? A poppy's red
In its barley bed.
What is blue? The sky is blue
Where the clouds float through.
What is white? A swan is white
Sailing in the light.
What is yellow? Pears are yellow,
Rich and ripe and mellow.
What is green? The grass is green
With small flowers between.
What is violet? Clouds are violet
In the summer twilight.
What is orange? Why, an orange –
Just an orange!

Colours

Frances Evans

Red is death, for people who are dying,
Silver is tears, for people who are crying,
Blue is a pool, cool and still,
Green is a beautiful grassy hill.

Grey is for people in the early evening,
Black is a dress for people grieving,
Brown is for an old queen's gown,
Gold for a princess's crown.

Sight

Wilfred Gibson

By the lamplight stall I loitered, feasting my eyes
On colours ripe and rich for the heart's desire –
Tomatoes redder than Krakatoa's fire,
Oranges like old sunsets over Tyre,
And apples golden-green as the glades of Paradise.

And as I lingered lost in divine delight,
My heart thanked God for the goodly gift of sight

     . . . . .
When suddenly behind me in the night
I heard the tapping of a blind man's stick.

Fire

James Reeves

Hard and black is my home,
Hard as rock and black as night.
Scarlet and gold am I,
Delicate, warm and bright.

For long years I lie,
A prisoner in the dark,
Till at last I break my fetters
In a rush of flame and spark.

First a tree and then a rock
The house where I sleep
Now like a demon
I crackle and hiss and leap.

November the Fifth

Leonard Clark

And you, big rocket,
   I watch how madly you fly
   Into the smoky sky
   With flaming tail;
   Hear your thin wail.

Catherine wheel,
   I see how fiercely you spin
   Round and round on your pin;
   How I admire
   Your circle of fire.

Roman candle,
   I watch how prettily you spark
   Stars in the autumn dark
   Falling like rain
   To shoot up again.

And you, old guy,
   I see how sadly you blaze on
   Till every scrap is gone;
   Burnt into ashes
   Your skeleton crashes.

And so,
   The happy ending of the fun,
   Fireworks over, bonfire done;
   Must wait a year now to remember
   Another fifth of November.

Symphony in Yellow

Oscar Wilde

An omnibus across the bridge
   Crawls like a yellow butterfly,
   And here and there, a passer-by
Shows like a little restless midge.

Big barges full of yellow hay
   Are moored against the shadowy wharf,
   And, like a yellow silken scarf,
The thick fog hangs along the quay.

The yellow leaves begin to fade
   And flutter from the Temple elms,
   And at my feet the pale green Thames
Lies like a rod of rippled jade.

Pleasant Sounds

John Clare

The rustling of leaves under the feet in woods and under
        hedges;
The crumpling of cat-ice and snow down wood-rides,
        narrow lanes, and every street causeway;
Rustling through a wood or rather rushing, while the wind
        halloos in the oak-top like thunder;
The rustle of birds' wings startled from their nests or flying
        unseen into the bushes;
The whizzing of larger birds overhead in a wood, such as
        crows, puddocks, buzzards;
The trample of robins and woodlarks on the brown leaves,
        and the patter of squirrels on the green moss;
The fall of an acorn on the ground, the pattering of nuts on
        the hazel branches as they fall from ripeness;
The flirt of the groundlark's wing from the stubbles – how
        sweet such pictures on dewy mornings, when
        the dew flashes from its brown feathers!

Noise

Jessie Pope

I like noise.
The whoop of a boy, the thud of a hoof,
The rattle of rain on a galvanised roof,
The hubbub of traffic, the roar of a train,
The throb of machinery numbing the brain,
The switching of wires in an overhead tram,
The rush of the wind, a door on the slam,
The boom of the thunder, the crash of the waves,
The din of a river that races and raves,
The crack of a rifle, the clank of a pail,
The strident tattoo of a swift slapping sail.
From any old sound that the silence destroys
Arises a gamut of soul-stirring joys.
I like noise.

Digging

Edward Thomas

To-day I think
Only with scents, – scents dead leaves yield,
And bracken, and wild carrot's seed,
And the square mustard field;

Odours that rise
When the spade wounds the root of tree,
Rose, currant, raspberry, or goutweed,
Rhubarb or celery;

The smoke's smell, too,
Flowing from where a bonfire burns
The dead, the waste, the dangerous,
And all to sweetness turns.

It is enough
To smell, to crumble the dark earth,
While the robin sings over again
Sad songs of Autumn mirth.

Sounds and Smells

J Charles

So many sounds bring delight;
The crunch of shoes on a frosty night,
The pouring of tea, the wind in the trees,
The swishing of cornfields in the breeze.

The joy of smells, too, will never pass;
I love the scent of new-mown grass,
The salty tang of a sandy beach,
And the gentle fragrance of a peach.

A Memory

Douglas Gibson

This I remember
I saw from a train
A shaggy wild pony
That stood in the rain.

Where I was going,
And where was the train,
I cannot remember,
I cannot explain.

All these years after
It comes back again:
A shaggy wild pony
That stood in the rain.

Anger

Yvonne Lowe (8)

I was angry and mad,
And it seemed that there was hot water inside me,
And as I got madder and madder,
The water got hotter and hotter all the time,
I was in a rage,
Then I began to see colours,
Like black and red,
Then as I got madder and madder,
My eyes began to pop out of my head,
They were popping up and down,
It was horrible,
And it would not stop,
I was steaming with anger,
Nobody could not stop me,
My mother could not stop me,
Then it was gone,
And I was all right,
Horrible, black, madness.

Angry

John Donald Williams (11)

You feel as if you could jump on them,
As if to kill them in anger,
It feels as if you had the strength,
Of a hundred men.
You get in a kind of a trance,
And go pushing people about,
The slightest thing that goes wrong,
Makes you blame it on someone else.
If a person gets angry with you,
You try not to listen.

Horrible Things

Roy Fuller

"What's the horriblest thing you've seen?"
Said Nell to Jean.

"Some grey-coloured, trodden-on Plasticine;
On a plate, a left-over cold baked bean;
A cloak-room ticket numbered thirteen;
A slice of meat without any lean;
The smile of a spiteful fairy-tale queen;
A thing in the sea like a brown submarine;
A cheese fur-coated in brilliant green;
A bluebottle perched on a piece of sardine.
What's the horriblest thing YOU'VE seen?"
Said Jean to Nell.

"Your face as you tell
Of all the horriblest things you've seen."

Jargon

James Reeves

Jerusalem, Joppa, Jericho –
These are the cities of long ago.

Jasper, Jacinth, jet and jade –
Of such are jewels for ladies made.

Juniper's green and jasmine's white.
Sweet jonquil is spring's delight.

Joseph, Jeremy, Jennifer, James,
Julian, Juliet – just names.

January, July and June –
Birthday late or birthday soon.

Jacket, jerkin, jersey, jeans –
What's the wear for sweet sixteens?

Jaguar, jackal, jumbo, jay –
Came to dinner but couldn't stay.

Jellies, junkets, jumbals, jam –
Mix them up for sweet-toothed Sam.

To jig, to jaunt, to jostle, to jest –
These are the things that Jack loves best.

Jazz, Jamboree, Jubilee, joke –
The jolliest words you ever spoke.

From A to Z and Z to A
The joyfullest letter of all is J.

The Big Rock Candy Mountains

Traditional American

On a summer's day in the month of May,
A burly bum came a-hiking,
Travelling down that lonesome road
A-looking for his liking.
He was headed for a land that was far away,
Beside them crystal fountains –
"I'll see you all this coming fall
In the Big Rock Candy Mountains."

In the Big Rock Candy Mountains
You never change your socks,
And little streams of alcohol
Come a-trickling down the rocks.
The box cars are all empty
And the railroad bulls are blind,
There's a lake of stew and whisky, too,
You can paddle all around 'em in a big canoe
In the Big Rock Candy Mountains.

O– the buzzing of the bees in the cigarette trees
Round the soda-water fountains,
Where the lemonade springs and the bluebird sings
In the Big Rock Candy Mountains.

In the Big Rock Candy Mountains,
There's a land that's fair and bright,
Where the hand-outs grow on bushes
And you sleep out every night,
Where the box cars are all empty
And the sun shines every day,
O I'm bound to go where there ain't no snow,
Where the rain don't fall and the wind don't blow
In the Big Rock Candy Mountains.

In the Big Rock Candy Mountains,
The jails are made of tin
And you can bust right out again
As soon as they put you in;
The farmers' trees are full of fruit,
The barns are full of hay,
I'm going to stay where you sleep all day,
Where they boiled in oil the inventor of toil
In the Big Rock Candy Mountains.

Sink Song

J A Lindon

Scouring out the porridge pot,
  Round and round and round!

Out with all the scraith and scoopery.
Lift the eely, ooly, droopery,
Chase the glubbery, slubbery, gloopery
  Round and round and round!

Out with all the doleful dithery,
Ladle out the slimy slithery,
Hunt and catch the hithery thithery
  Round and round and round!

Out with all the obbly gubbly,
On the stove it burns so bubbly,
Use the spoon and use it doubly,
  Round and round and round!

Sewing Machine

Gwen Dunn

I'm faster, I'm faster than fingers,
        much faster.
No mistress can match me, no mistress
        nor master.
My bobbin is racing to feed in the
        thread,
Pink, purple, grey, green, lemon-yellow,
        or red.
My needle, my needle, my slim, sharp
        steel needle,
Makes tiny, neat stitches in trousers
        and dresses
And firmly my silver foot presses,
        it presses.
I'm faster, I'm faster than fingers,
        much faster.

What is the Grass?

Walt Whitman

A child said, "What is the grass?" fetching it to me with full
        hands;
How could I answer the child? I do not know what it is any
        more than he.

Phizzog

Carl Sandburg

This face you got,
This here phizzog you carry around,
You never picked it out for yourself, at all, at all, – did you?
This here phizzog – Somebody handed it to you – am I
        right?
Somebody said, "Here's yours, now go see what you can
        do with it."
Somebody slipped it to you and it was like a package
        marked:
"No goods exchanged after being taken away" –
This face you got.

Fish and Chips

L T Baynton

Heading for the light, bitter cold night,
Round this corner – smell it now?
Windows steamed like fog inside.
Hungry queue all bags in hands.
Old papers piled but not to read,
Giant sized salt and vinegar near,
And wooden forks like babies toys.
Nearer now, oh hear the hiss,
And on the shelf the golden plaice, the chips.
At last my turn, my mouth is wet –
No thanks, not wrapped – hot in my hand.
Outside the night seems warmer now,
Until – I hold a crumpled paper ball
Why do they go so soon?

As

Anon

As wet as a fish – as dry as a bone;
As live as a bird – as dead as a stone;
As plump as a partridge – as poor as a rat;
As strong as a horse – as weak as a cat;
As hard as flint – as soft as a mole;
As white as a lily – as black as coal;
As plain as a pike-staff – as rough as a bear;
As tight as a drum – as free as the air;
As heavy as lead – as light as a feather;
As steady as time – uncertain as weather;
As hot as a furnace – as cold as a frog;
As gay as a lark – as sick as a dog;
As slow as a tortoise – as swift as the wind;
As true as the gospel – as false as mankind;
As thin as a herring – as fat as a pig;
As proud as a peacock – as blithe as a jig;
As fierce as a tiger – as mild as a dove;
As stiff as a poker – as limp as a glove;
As blind as a bat – as deaf as a post;
As cool as a cucumber – as warm as toast;
As flat as a flounder – as round as a ball;
As blunt as a hammer – as sharp as an awl;
As red as a ferret – as safe as the stocks;
As bold as a thief – as sly as a fox;
As straight as an arrow – as bent as a bow;
As yellow as saffron – as black as a sloe;
As brittle as glass – as tough as gristle;
As neat as my nail – as clean as a whistle;
As good as a feast – as bad as a witch;

As light as is day – as dark as is pitch;
As brisk as a bee – as dull as an ass;
As full as a tick – as solid as brass.

Little Girl

Rose Fyleman

I will build you a house
If you do not cry,
A house, little girl,
As tall as the sky.

I will build you a house
Of golden dates,
The freshest of all
For the steps and gates.

I will furnish the house,
For you and for me
With walnuts and hazels
Fresh from the tree.

I will build you a house,
And when it is done
I will roof it with grapes
To keep out the sun.

This Old Hammer

Traditional American

This old hammer
Shine like silver,
Shine like gold, boys
Shine like gold.

Well don't you hear that
Hammer ringing?
Drivin' in steel, boys,
Drivin' in steel.

Can't find a hammer
On this old mountain,
Rings like mine, boys,
Rings like mine.

I've been working
On this old mountain
Seven long years, boys,
Seven long years.

I'm going back to
Swannanoa Town-o,
That's my home, boys,
That's my home.

Take this hammer,
Give it to the captain.
Tell him I'm gone, boys,
Tell him I'm gone.

The Scarecrow

Michael Franklin

A scarecrow stood in a field one day,
        Stuffed with straw,
        Stuffed with hay;
He watched the folk on the king's highway,
  But never a word said he.

Much he saw but naught did heed,
        Knowing not night,
        Knowing not day,
For, having nought, did nothing need,
  And never a word said he.

A little grey mouse had made its nest,
        Oh so wee,
        Oh so grey,
In a sleeve of a coat that was poor Tom's best,
  But the scarecrow naught said he.

His hat was the home of a small jenny wren,
        Ever so sweet,
        Ever so gay,
A squirrel had put by his fear of men,
  And kissed him, but naught heeded he.

Ragged old man, I loved him well,
        Stuffed with straw,
        Stuffed with hay,
Many's the tale that he could tell,
  But never a word says he.

The Song the Train Sang

Neil Adams

Now
When the
Steam hisses;
Now when the
Coupling clashes;
Now
When the
Wind rushes,
Comes the slow but sudden swaying,
Every truck and carriage trying
For a smooth and better rhythm,
For a smooth and singing rhythm.

This . . . is . . . the . . . one . . .
That . . . is . . . the . . . one . . .
This is the one,
That is the one,
This is the one, that is the one,
This is the one, that is the one.

Over the river, past the mill,
Through the tunnel under the hill;
Round the corner, past the wall,
Through the wood where trees grow tall,
Then in sight of the town by the river,
Brake by the crossing where white leaves quiver.
Slow as the streets of the town slide past
As the windows stare at the jerking of the coaches
Coming into the station approaches.

Stop at the front.
Stop at the front.
Stop . . . at the front.
Stop . . . at the . . .
Stop.
    AHHHH!

Engine No. 9

Anon

Engine, engine, number nine,
Sliding down Chicago line;
When she's polished she will shine,
Engine, engine, number nine.

Button Box

Leonard Clark

An evening of wind and rain,
I found it on a shelf,
The button box, so full
Its lid would barely stay closed,
And opened it. Buttons.
Took them out one by one, all different
Shapes, sizes, colours, dull, thin;
Bone sometimes, and metal,
Holes, and none, some chipped,
A few leather, one had head of fox,
Another would do for dwarf's shield;
A dozen mother-of-pearl sang of the sea.
A set of silver ones
Might have been sixpences dancing.
A jet-black handful
Went to grandfather's funeral, two
Only from mother's wedding dress,
Tiny, pink as rosebuds.
I turned them over and over, those buttons,
Our family there, laid out in rows,
Dotting the table, reflections in lamplight,
Then put them back, boy, girl,
Man, woman, warm from my fingers,
Into their cramped box,
Counted raindrops.

MAIN DEEP

The Sea Serpent Chantey

Vachel Lindsay

There's a snake on the western wave
And his crest is red.
He is long as a city street,
And he eats the dead.
There's a hole in the bottom of the sea
Where the snake goes down.
And he waits in the bottom of the sea
For the men that drown.

Chorus   This is the voice of the sand
           (The sailors understand)
           "There is far more sea than sand,
           There is far more sea than land.
           Yo . . . ho, yo . . . ho."

He waits by the door of his cave
While the ages moan.
He cracks the ribs of the ships
With his teeth of stone.
In his gizzard deep and long
Much treasure lies.
Oh, the pearls and the Spanish gold . . .
And the idols' eyes . . .
Oh, the totem poles . . . the skulls . . .
The altars cold . . .
The wedding rings, the dice . . .
The buoy bells old.

Chorus   This is the voice of the sand
          (The sailors understand)
          "There is far more sea than sand,
          There is far more sea than land.
          Yo . . . ho, yo . . . ho."

Dive, mermaids, with sharp swords
And cut him through,
And bring us the idols' eyes
And the red gold too.
Lower the grappling hooks
Good pirate men
And drag him up by the tongue
From his deep wet den.

Repeat as a second chorus many times.
          We will sail to the end of the world,
          We will nail his hide
          To the mainmast of the moon
          In the evening tide.

Or will you let him live,
The deep-sea thing,
With the wrecks of all the world
In a black wide ring
By the hole in the bottom of the sea
Where the snake goes down,
Where he waits in the bottom of the sea
For the men that drown?

Chorus   This is the voice of the sand
          (The sailors understand)
          "There is far more sea than sand,
          There is far more sea than land.
          Yo . . . ho, yo . . . ho!"

The Fisherman's Boats

Annie Wrench

When the tide ebbs
   And the sands are dry,
The fishermen's boats
   All resting lie.

When the tide flows
   As it turns once more,
And fills with its waters
   The bay's wide shore,

While wild sea-horses
   Around them prance,
The fishermen's boats
   All rock and dance.

The tide rises, the tide falls

Henry Wadsworth Longfellow

The tide rises, the tide falls,
The twilight darkens, the curlew calls;
Along the sea – sands damp and brown
The traveller hastens towards the town;
   And the tide rises, the tide falls.

Darkness settles on roofs and walls,
But the sea in the darkness calls and calls;
The little waves, with their soft white hands
Efface the footprints in the sands,
   And the tide rises, the tide falls.

The morning breaks; the steeds in their stalls,
Stamp and neigh, as the ostler calls;
The day returns; but nevermore
Returns the traveller to the shore,
   And the tide rises, the tide falls.

Grim and Gloomy

James Reeves

Oh, grim and gloomy,
So grim and gloomy
Are the caves beneath the sea.
Oh, rare but roomy
And bare and boomy,
Those salt sea caverns be.

Oh, slim and slimy
Or grey and grimy
Are the animals of the sea.
Salt and oozy
And safe and snoozy
The caves where those animals be.

Hark to the shuffling,
Huge and snuffling,
Ravenous, cavernous, great sea-beasts!
But fair and fabulous,
Tintinnabulous,
Gay and fabulous are their feasts.

Ah, but the queen of the sea,
The querulous, perilous sea!
How the curls of her tresses
The pearls on her dresses,
Sway and swirl in the waves,
How cosy and dozy,
How sweet ring a-rosy
Her bower in the deep-sea caves!

Oh, rare but roomy
And bare and boomy
Those caverns under the sea,
And grave and grandiose
Safe and sandiose
The dens of her denizens be.

From The Ballad of the Kon-Tiki

Ian Serraillier

Then did Ocean,
The great showman, out of the bountiful deep
Conjure all manner of strange creatures
To delight them: flying fish that shot through the air
Like quicksilver, smack against the sail,
Then dropped to deck into the breakfast saucepan
Waiting there; the prosperous tunny,
Fat as an alderman with rows of double chins;
The glorious dolphin, blue-bottle green,
With glittering golden fins, greedy
For the succulent weed that trailed like garlands
From the steering oar. There were many more –
Take the blue shark, a glutton
For blood: he'd swallow a dolphin, bones and all,
And crunch them like a concrete-mixer.

Horses

Christina Rossetti

The horses of the sea
   Rear a foaming crest,
But the horses of the land
   Serve us the best.

The horses of the land
   Munch corn and clover,
While the foaming sea-horses
   Toss and turn over.

The Lighthouse

Enid Madoc-Jones

The sun's last light has gone,
The night has veiled the trees;
Has hid the road that winds beyond
The roof-tops and the eaves.

There is no moon or star,
No guiding lamp to gleam,
Only the lighthouse, standing far,
Swings high one level beam.

The Sea

James Reeves

The sea is a hungry dog,
Giant and grey.
He rolls on the beach all day.
With his clashing teeth and shaggy jaws
Hour upon hour he gnaws
The rumbling, tumbling, stones,
And "Bones, bones, bones, bones!"
The giant sea-dog moans,
Licking his greasy paws.

And when the night wind roars
And the moon rocks in the stormy cloud,
He bounds to his feet and snuffs and sniffs,
Shaking his wet sides over the cliffs,
And howls and hollows long and loud.

But on quiet days in May or June,
When even the grasses on the dune
Play no more their reedy tune,
With his head between his paws
He lies on the sandy shores,
So quiet, so quiet, he scarcely snores.

The Diver

Ian Serraillier

I put on my aqua-lung and plunge,
Exploring, like a ship with a glass keel,
The secrets of the deep. Along my lazy road
On and on I steal –
Over waving bushes which at a touch explode
Into shrimps, then closing, rock to the tune of the tide;
Over crabs that vanish in puffs of sand.
Look, a string of pearls bubbling at my side
Breaks in my hand –
Those pearls were my breath . . . Does that hollow hide
Some old Armada wreck in seaweed furled,
Crusted with barnacles, her cannon rusted,
The great *San Philip*? What bullion in her hold?
Pieces of eight, silver crowns, and bars of solid gold?

I shall never know. Too soon the clasping cold
Fastens on flesh and limb
And pulls me to the surface. Shivering, back I swim
To the beach, the noisy crowds, the ordinary world.

Sea Shell

Enid Madoc-Jones

Lift to your ear
The gleaming wave-washed shell,
Its song may tell
Strange ocean fantasies
Of silver pearls,
Glimpsed through the restless surge,
Of slender sinous weeds
That golden patterns weave
By banks of bright anemones;
Of fishes, rainbow finned;
Of secret twilight caves,
Where tides, their fury tamed,
Go stealing tip-toe in.

There are big waves

Eleanor Farjeon

There are big waves and little waves,
Green waves and blue,
Waves you can jump over,
Waves you dive through.

Waves that rise up
Like a great water wall,
Waves that swell softly
And don't break at all.

Waves that can whisper,
Waves that can roar,
And tiny waves that run at you
Running on the shore.

Sam

Walter de la Mare

When Sam goes back in memory,
   It is to where the sea
Breaks on the shingle, emerald-green,
   In white foam, endlessly;
He says – with small brown eye on mine –
   "I used to keep awake,
And lean from my window in the moon,
   Watching those billows break.
And half a million tiny hands,
   And eyes, like sparks of frost,
Would dance and come tumbling into the moon,
   On every breaker tossed.
And all across from star to star,
   I've seen the watery sea,
With not a single ship in sight,
   Just ocean there, and me;
And heard my father snore. . . And once,
   As sure as I'm alive,
Out of those wallowing, moon-flecked waves
   I saw a mermaid dive;
Head and shoulders above the wave,
   Plain as I now see you,
Combing her hair, now back, now front,
   Her two eyes peeping through;
Calling me, "Sam!" – quietlike – "Sam!" . . .
   But me . . . I never went,
Making believe I kind of thought
   'Twas someone else she meant . . .
Wonderful lovely there she sat,

Singing the night away,
All in the solitudinous sea
    Of that there lonely bay.
"P'raps," and he'd smooth his hairless mouth,
    "P'raps, if 'twere *now*, my son,
P'raps, if I heard a voice say, 'Sam!' . . .
    Morning would find me gone."

Lightships

Clive Sansom

All night long when the wind is high
Nnn nnn nnnn
The lightships moan and moan to the sky
Nnn nnn nnnn.

Their foghorns whine when the mist runs free
Nnn nnn nnnn
Warning the men on the ships at sea
Nnn nnn nnnn.

Off the Ground

Walter de la Mare

Three jolly Farmers
Once bet a pound
Each dance the other would
Off the ground.
Out of their coats
They slipped right soon,
And neat and nicesome,
Put each his shoon.

One – Two – Three! –
And away they go,
Not too fast,
And not too slow;
Out from the elm-tree's
Noonday shadow,
Into the sun
And across the meadow.
Past the schoolroom,
With knees well bent
Fingers a-flicking,
They dancing went.
Up sides and over,
And round and round,
They crossed click-clacking,
The Parish bound.
By Tupman's meadow
They did their mile,
Tee-to-tum
On a three-barred stile.
Then straight through Whipham,

Downhill to Week,
Footing it lightsome
But not too quick,
Up fields to Watchet,
And on through Wye,
Till seven fine churches
They'd seen skip by –
Seven fine churches,
And five old mills,
Farms in the valley,
And sheep on the hills;
Old Man's Acre
And Dead Man's Pool
All left behind,
As they danced through Wool.

And Wool gone by,
Like tops that seem
To spin in sleep
They dance in dream:
Withy – Wellover –
Wassop – Wo –
Like an old clock
Their heels did go.
A league and a league
And a league they went,
And not one weary,
And not one spent.
And lo, and behold!
Past Willow-cum-Leigh
Stretched with its waters
The great green sea.

Says Farmer Bates,
"I puffs and I blows,
What's under the water,
Why, no man knows."
Says Farmer Giles,
"My wind comes weak
And a good man drowned
Is far to seek."
But Farmer Turvey
On twirling toes
Ups with his gaiters
And in he goes:
Down where the mermaids
Pluck and play
On their twangling harps
In a sea-green day;
Down where the mermaids
Finned and fair,
Sleek with their combs
Their yellow hair . . .

Bates and Giles —
On the shingle sat,
Gazing at Turvey's
Floating hat.
But never a tipple
Nor bubble told
Where he was supping
Off plates of gold.
Never an echo
Rilled through the sea
Of the feasting and dancing
And minstrelsy.
They called — called — called:

Came no reply:
Nought but the ripples'
Sandy sigh.
Then glum and silent
They sat instead,
Vacantly brooding
On home and bed,
Till both together
Stood up and said: –
"Us know not, dreams not,
Where you be,
Turvey, unless
In the deep blue sea;
But axcusing silver –
And it comes most willing –
Here's us two paying
Our forty shilling;
For it's sartin sure, Turvey,
Safe and sound,
You danced us square, Turvey;
Off the ground!"

The Sharks

Denise Levertov

Well, then, the last day the sharks appeared.
Dark fins appear, innocent
as if in fair warning. The sea becomes
sinister, are they everywhere?
I tell you, they break six feet of water.
Isn't it the same sea, and won't we
play in it any more?
I liked it clear and not
too calm, enough waves
to fly in on. For the first time
I dared to swim out of my depth.
It was sundown when they came, the time
When a sheen of copper stills the sea,
not dark enough for moonlight, clear enough
to see them easily. Dark
the sharp lift of the fins.

Sea Dirge

From The Tempest

William Shakespeare

Full fathom five thy father lies;
Of his bones are coral made;
Those are pearls that were his eyes:
Nothing of him that doth fade
But doth suffer a sea-change
Into something rich and strange.
Sea-nymphs hourly ring his knell.
Hark! now I hear them, – Ding-dong, bell.

Summer Song

John Ciardi

By the sand between my toes,
By the waves behind my ears,
By the sunburn on my nose,
By the little salty tears
That make rainbows in the sun
When I squeeze my eyes and run,
By the way the seagulls screech,
Guess where I am? *At the* . . . .!
By the way the children shout
Guess what happened? *School is* . . . . .!
By the way I sing this song
Guess if summer lasts too long:
You must answer *Right or* . . . .!

Seven Fat Fishermen

Anon

Seven fat fishermen,
Sitting side by side,
Fished from a bridge,
By the banks of the Clyde.

The first caught a tiddler,
The second caught a crab,
The third caught a winkle,
The fourth caught a dab.

The fifth caught a tadpole,
The sixth caught an eel,
But the seventh, he caught
An old cartwheel.

Coral

Christina Rossetti

O sailor, come ashore,
    What have you brought for me?
Red coral, white coral,
    Coral from the sea

I did not dig it from the ground,
    Nor pluck it from a tree;
Feeble insects made it
    In the stormy sea.

Old Man Ocean

Russell Hoban

Old man Ocean, how do you pound
Smooth glass rough, rough stones round?
    Time and tide and the wild waves rolling,
    Night and the wind and the long grey dawn.

Old man Ocean, what do you tell,
What do you sing in the empty shell?
    Fog and the storm and the long bell tolling,
    Bones in the deep and the brave men gone.

The Jumblies

Edward Lear

They went to sea in a Sieve, they did,
   In a Sieve they went to sea:
In spite of all their friends could say,
   On a winter's morn, on a stormy day,
In a Sieve they went to sea!
   And when the Sieve turned round and round,
And everyone cried, "You'll all be drowned!"
   They called aloud, "Our Sieve ain't big,
But we don't care a button! We don't care a fig!
   In a Sieve we'll go to sea!"
Far and few, far and few,
   Are the lands where the Jumblies live;
Their heads are green, and their hands are blue,
   And they went to sea in a Sieve.

They sailed away in a Sieve, they did,
   In a Sieve they sailed so fast,
With only a beautiful pea-green veil
   Tied with a riband by way of a sail,
To a small tobacco-pipe mast;
   And everyone said, who saw them go,
"Oh won't they be soon upset you know!
   For the sky is dark, and the voyage is long,
And happen what may, it's extremely wrong
   In a Sieve to sail so fast!"
Far and few, far and few,
   Are the lands where the Jumblies live;
Their heads are green, and their hands are blue,
   And they went to sea in a Sieve.

The water it soon came in, it did,
   The water it soon came in;
So to keep them dry, they wrapped their feet
   In a pinky paper all folded neat,
And they fastened it down with a pin.
   And they passed the night in a crockery-jar,
And each of them said, "How wise we are!
   Though the sky be dark, and the voyage be long,
Yet we never can think we were rash or wrong,
   While round in our Sieve we spin!"
Far and few, far and few,
   Are the lands where the Jumblies live;
Their heads are green, and their hands are blue,
   And they went to sea in a Sieve.

And all night long they sailed away;
   And when the sun went down,
They whistled and warbled a moony song
   To the echoing sound of a coppery gong,
In the shade of the mountains brown.
   "O Timballo! How happy we are,
When we live in a Sieve and a crockery-jar,
   And all night long in the moonlight pale,
We sail away with a pea-green sail,
   In the shade of the mountains brown!"
Far and few, far and few,
   Are the lands where the Jumblies live;
Their heads are green, and their hands are blue,
   And they went to sea in a Sieve.

They sailed to the Western Sea, they did,
   To a land all covered with trees,
And they bought an Owl, and a useful Cart,
   And a pound of Rice and a Cranberry Tart,

And a hive of silvery Bees.
    And they bought a Pig, and some green Jackdaws,
And a lovely Monkey with lollipop paws,
    And forty bottles of Ring-Bo-Ree,
And no end of Stilton cheese.
    Far and few, far and few,
Are the lands where the Jumblies live;
    Their heads are green, and their hands are blue,
And they went to sea in a Sieve.

And in twenty years they all came back,
    In twenty years or more,
And everyone said, "How tall they've grown!
    For they've been to the Lakes, and the Torrible Zone,
And the hills of the Chankly Bore;"
    And they drank their health, and gave them a feast
Of dumplings made of beautiful yeast;
    And everyone said, "If we only live,
We too will go to sea in a Sieve –
    To the hills of the Chankly Bore!"
Far and few, far and few,
    Are the lands where the Jumblies live;
Their heads are green, and their hands are blue,
    And they went to sea in a Sieve.

The Whale

Buson

Japanese poem translated by H G Henderson

A whale!
   Down it goes, and more and more,
      up goes its tail!

The Main-Deep

James Stephens

The long-rólling
Steady-póuring
Deep-trenchéd
Green billów:

The wide-topped,
Unbróken,
Green-glacid,
Slow-sliding,

Cold-flushing,
– On – on– on,
Chill-rushing,
Hush-hushing,

. . . Hush-hushing . . .

WHAT IF THE HILLS SHOULD STIR?

The Hills

Rachel Field

Sometimes I think the hills
That loom across the harbour
Lie there like sleeping dragons,
Crouched one above another,
With trees for tufts of fur
Growing all up and down
The ridges and humps of their backs,
And orange cliffs for claws
Dipped in the sea below.
Sometimes a wisp of smoke
Rises out of the hollows,
As if in their dragon sleep
They dreamed of strange old battles.

What if the hills should stir
Some day and stretch themselves,
Shake off the clinging trees
And all the clustered houses?

Tramp Tree

Anthony Barton (9)

The tree with braces 'angin' out
Like rags of a Tramp.
When the tree sways in the wind
    It's like a tramp's arm with hairs on.
Their fingers at the top of the tree,
Their tearing fingers,
Tearing holes in the sky,
Try to grab what isn't there
Trying to get free.
Spiky grass in his hair
And half his head is under the grass
With his brain as dirt
The roots are like veins
Pulled out with the strength of his arms
His body with worms all wriggling about
Keeping him down
The stones that he eats
Fall down his throat
And stop at an end.

All Change

Libby Houston

All change! All change!

When the guard on the train
or the bus conductor
shouts "All change!"
and everyone has to grab their things
in a terrible fluster
and get out again –
just suppose
he was a magician in disguise
having a joke! –
and the moment he spoke,
suddenly all the mums and dads
with their papers and cases and shopping-bags,
the school-children, workmen and office-girls neat
did change! –
and found themselves
out in the street
like a runaway zoo,
with a bear or two,
a tiger, a goat, a wasp and a frog,
pigs, crows, snakes and a kangaroo-dog,
an alligator, a chimpanzee –
and a few left behind on board –
a sunflower,
a couple of stones
and a tree –

What do you think you'd be?

Which?

Leonard Clark

Would you rather be
Thin
as
a
Pin
or
Lean
as
a
Sardine?
Or do you agree
It would be better if you were as Thick as an old oak tree,
Fat as a pig, or harvest pumpkin, or dusty honey bee?

O dear me, no,
I don't want to become
Tiny like Tom Thumb
or grow
Small enough to live with a mouse
in his house;

I don't want to be as Big as an elephant, Wider than a bus,
Huge as a fairy tale giant or a hippopotamus,
I think I'd rather stay
Just as I am if I may,
The same size tomorrow as yesterday.

In my new clothing

Basho

Translated by H G Henderson

In my new clothing
   I feel so different
   I must
Look like someone else.

Tender-heartedness

Harry Graham

Billy in one of his nice new sashes,
Fell in the fire and was burnt to ashes;
Now, although the room grows chilly,
I haven't the heart to poke poor Billy.

Little Old Man

Charlotte Zolotow

Little old man hunched and grey
I know you were young once – like me.
But it's hard to believe I'll ever be
the way I see you are today
hunched and grey
little old man
(once young like me)

Imagine

Roland Egan

Imagine a snail
As big as a whale,
Imagine a lark
As big as a shark,
Imagine a cat
As small as a gnat
And a bee as big as a tree.

Imagine a toad
As long as a road,
Imagine a hare
As big as a chair,
Imagine a goat
As long as a boat
And a flea the same size as me.

Night Starvation or The Biter Bit

Carey Blyton

At night, my Uncle Rufus
(Or so I've heard it said)
Would put his teeth into a glass
Of water by his bed.

At three o'clock one morning
He woke up with a cough,
And as he reached out for his teeth –
They bit his hand right off.

How Strange

Charlotte Zolotow

How strange when I finally die
to lie beneath the grass and snow
while overhead the birds fly by
and I can't watch them go.

The Pedalling Man

Russell Hoban

We put him on the roof and we painted him blue,
And the pedalling man knew what to do—
He just pedalled, yes he pedalled:
He rode through the night with the wind just right
And he rode clear into the morning,
Riding easy, riding breezy, riding
Slow in the sunrise and the wind out of the east.

A weathervane was what he was—
Cast-iron man with a sheet-iron propeller, riding a
Worm gear, holding a little steering wheel,
Iron legs pumping up and down – show him a
Wind and he'd go. Work all day and
All his pay was the weather. Nights, too,
We'd lie in bed and hear him
Creak up there in the dark as he
Swung into the wind and worked up speed,
Humming and thrumming so you could
Feel it all through the house—
The more wind, the faster he went, right through
Spring, summer and fall.

He rode warm winds out of the south,
Wet winds out of the east, and the
Dry west winds, rode them all with a
Serious iron face. Hard-nosed, tight-mouthed
Yankee-looking kind of an iron man.
"Show me a wind and I'll go," he said.
"I'm a pedalling fool and I'm heading for weather."
The weather came and he kept on going, right into
Winter, and the wind out of the north and no let up—
We lived on a hill, and wind was what we got a lot of.

Then a night came along, and a blizzard was making,
Windows rattling and the whole house shaking,
But the iron man just hummed with the blast,
Said, "Come on, wind, and come on fast,
Show me your winter, make it nice and cool,
Show me your weather – I'm a pedalling fool!"
Gears all spinning, joints all shivering,
Sheet-iron clattering, cast-iron quivering till WHOMP!
The humming stopped, and we all sat up in bed with
Nothing to listen to but the wind right through into
            morning.

And there he was when we dug him out, propeller all bent,
One eye in the snow and one eye
Staring up at the sky, still looking for weather.
He never let on he was beat, not him.

Well, my father put him up on the roof again, this time
Without the propeller.
"Let him ride easy," he said. "A man can only take
Just so much north wind, even if he's iron."

The Bulldozer

Stanley Cook

An orange-coated man
Who wears for his work
The colour of coat
You see in the dark
Starts the engine
Bang-b-bang-bang.

The bulldozer scoop
Is like a boot
As if a giant
Smoothed the ground
With the side of his foot
Down-d-down-down.

Digging its tracks
Into the mud
The yellow bulldozer
Bends its back
Like a butting bull
Charge-ch-charge-thud.

It lifts loose earth
Away from its feet
And drops it in a heap
Or dumps it in a truck
Bump-b-bump-full.

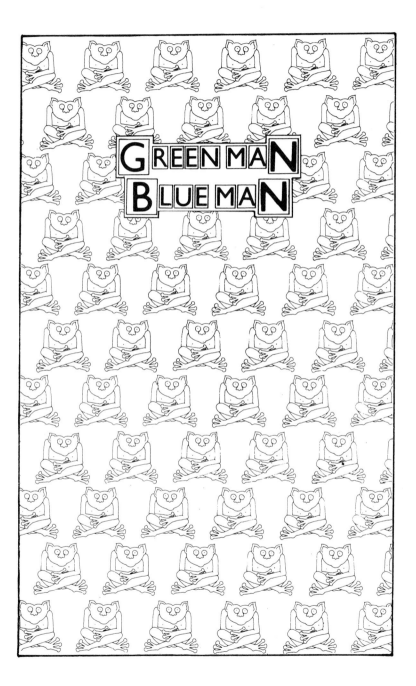

Fat Old Witch

Leland B Jacobs

The strangest sight
I've ever seen
Was a fat old witch
In a flying machine.

The witch flew high,
The witch flew low,
The witch flew fast,
The witch flew slow,
The witch flew up,
The witch flew down,
She circled all
Around the town.
Then, turning left,
And turning right,
She disappeared into the night.

That fat old witch
In a flying machine
Is the strangest sight
I've ever seen.
Of course it happened
On Hallowe'en.

Space Travellers

James Nimmo

There was a witch, hump-backed and hooded,
   Lived by herself in a burnt-out tree.
When storm winds shrieked and the moon was buried
   And the dark of the forest was black as black,
She rose in the air like a rocket at sea,
   Riding the wind,
   Riding the night,
Riding the tempest to the moon and back.

There may be a man with a hump of silver,
   Telescope eyes and a telephone ear,
Dials to twist and knobs to twiddle,
   Waiting for a night when skies are clear,
To shoot from the scaffold with a blazing track,
   Riding the dark,
   Riding the cold,
Riding the silence to the moon and back.

Green Man, Blue Man

Charles Causley

As I was walking through Guildhall Square
I smiled to see a green man there,
But when I saw him coming near
My heart was filled with nameless fear.

As I was walking through Madford Lane
A blue man stood there in the rain.
I asked him in by my front-door,
For I'd seen a blue man before.

As I was walking through Landlake Wood
A grey man in the forest stood,
But when he turned and said, "Good day"
I shook my head and ran away.

As I was walking by Church Stile
A purple man spoke there a while.
I spoke to him because, you see,
A purple man once lived by me.

But when the night falls dark and fell
How, O how, am I to tell,
Grey man, green man, purple, blue,
Which is which is which of you?

The Penny Fiddle

Robert Graves

Yesterday I bought a penny fiddle
   And put it to my chin to play;
But I found that the strings were painted
   So I threw my fiddle away.

A little red man found my fiddle
   As it lay abandoned there,
He asked me if he might keep it,
   And I told him I did not care.

But he drew such music from the fiddle
   With help of a farthing bow
That I offered five guineas for the secret
   But alas, he would never let it go.

The Hairy Toe

Traditional American

Once there was a woman went out to pick beans,
and she found a Hairy Toe.
She took the Hairy Toe home with her,
and that night, when she went to bed,
the wind began to moan and groan.
Away off in the distance
she seemed to hear a voice crying,
"Where's my Hair-r-ry To-o-oe?
Who's got my Hair-r-ry To-o-oe?"

The woman scrooched down,
way down under the covers,
and about that time
the wind appeared to hit the house,

smoosh,

and the old house creaked and cracked
like something was trying to get in.
The voice had come nearer,
almost at the door now,
and it said,
"Where's my Hair-r-ry To-o-oe?
Who's got my Hair-r-ry To-o-oe?"

The woman scrooched further down
under the covers
and pulled them tight around her head.

The wind growled around the house
like some big animal
and r-r-um-mbled
over the chimbley.
All at once she heard the door cr-r-a-ack
and Something slipped in
and began to creep over the floor.

The floor went
cre-e-eak, cre-e-eak
at every step that thing took towards her bed.
The woman could almost feel it
bending over her bed.
Then in an awful voice it said:
"Where's my Hair-r-ry To-o-oe?
Who's got my Hair-r-ry To-o-oe?
You've got it!"

At the Keyhole

Walter de la Mare

"Grill me some bones," said the Cobbler,
    "Some bones, my pretty Sue;
I'm tired of my lonesome with heels and soles
Springsides and uppers too;
A mouse in the wainscot is nibbling;
A wind in the keyhole drones;
And a sheet webbed over my candle, Susie –
    Grill me some bones!"

"Grill me some bones," said the Cobbler,
    "I sat at my tic-tac-to;
And a footstep came to my door and stopped,
And a hand groped to and fro;
And I peered up over my boot and last;
And my feet went cold as stones:–
I saw an eye at the keyhole, Susie –
    Grill me some bones!"

hist whist

e e cummings

hist whist
little ghostthings
tip-toe
twinkle-toe

little twitchy
witches and tingling
goblins
hob-a-nob hob-a-nob

little hoppy happy
toad in tweeds
tweeds
little itchy mousies

with scuttling
eyes   rustle and run   and
hidehidehide
whisk

whisk   look out for the old woman
with the wart on her nose
what she'll do to yer
nobody knows

for she knows the devil   ooch
the devil   ouch
the devil
ach   the great

green
dancing
devil
devil

devil
devil

wheeEEE

The Listeners

Walter de la Mare

"Is there anybody there?" said the Traveller,
    Knocking on the moonlit door;
And his horse in the silence champed the grasses
    Of the forest's ferny floor:
And a bird flew up out of the turret,
    Above the Traveller's head:
And he smote upon the door again a second time;
    "Is there anybody there?" he said.
But no one descended to the Traveller;
    No head from the leaf-fringed sill
Leaned over and looked into his grey eyes,
    Where he stood perplexed and still.
But only a host of phantom listeners
    That dwelt in the lone house then
Stood listening in the quiet of moonlight
    To that voice from the world of men:
Stood thronging the faint moonbeams on the dark stair
    That goes down to the empty hall,
Hearkening in an air stirred and shaken
    By the lonely Traveller's call.
And he felt in his heart their strangeness,
    Their stillness answering his cry,
While his horse moved, cropping the dark turf,
    'Neath the starred and leafy sky;
For he suddenly smote on the door, even
    Louder, and then lifted his head:
"Tell them I came, and no one answered,
    That I kept my word," he said.
Never the least stir made the listeners,

Though every word he spake
Fell echoing through the shadowiness of the still house
    From the one man left awake:
Ay, they heard his foot upon the stirrup,
    And the sound of iron on stone,
And how the silence surged softly backward,
    When the plunging hoofs were gone.

The Witch! The Witch!

Eleanor Farjeon

The Witch! The Witch! Don't let her get you!
Or your Aunt wouldn't know you the next time she met
                you!

The Ballad of the Carpenters

L A G Strong

An ancient woman met with me,
Her voice was silver as her hair,
Her wild black eyes were certainly
The strangest I have seen.
She told a tale of carpenters
Who laboured for a queen.

"I had an island in a lake,
A wide lake, a quiet lake
Of sweet security.
I called them to me by the lake,
And they came gladly for my sake, –
My seven singing carpenters,
To build a house for me.

"They brought the hammer and the nails,
The pegs, the twine, the chisel blade,
The saw and whizzing plane.
They brought good share of timber wood,
Of resin wood, sweet smelling wood
Split kindly to the grain.
They brought them all for love of me;
They did not seek for gain.

"They built a house of singing wood, –
The white wood, the splendid wood, –
And made it snug around.
Their hammers on the ringing wood
Made all the lake resound.

"The tench stirred dimly in his dream,
The glowing carp, the silly bream
Could hear the muffled sound.

"But someone grudged the fragrant wood
And sent a storm upon my house,
A black flood, a silver flood
Of wind and stinging rain.
The waters writhed in hissing rage,
The yelling wind, the rain-pocked waves
Rose in a hurricane.

"The slaty waves foamed hillock high,
The thunder pranced about the sky,
The lightning's bare and crooked fang
Gleamed where the cloud-lip curled.

"And when the calm came, and the peace
Of wind's cease and water's cease,
My house and seven carpenters
Had vanished from the world."

Overheard on a Salt Marsh

Harold Monro

Nymph, nymph, what are your beads?
Green glass, goblin. Why do you stare at them?
Give them me.
              No
Give them me. Give them me.
                          No.
Then I will howl all night in the reeds,
Lie in the mud and howl for them.

Goblin, why do you love them so?

They are better than stars or water,
Better than voices of winds that sing,
Better than any man's fair daughter,
Your green glass beads on a silver ring.

Hush, I stole them out of the moon.

Give me your beads, I want them.
                        No.
I will howl in a deep lagoon
For your green glass beads, I love them so.
Give them me. Give them.
                    No.

The Sorcerer's Apprentice

Martin Brennan

One day a sorcerer left his den
In charge of his apprentice;
This was a foolish thing for when
The boy found himself alone
He read a book of magic spells
And turned the big black cat to stone.
He made the long broom sweep the floor
Brush a brush a wisk a wisk
He made the hard brush scrub the floor
Scrub a rub, scrub a rub,
Scrubbity rubbity rub rub,
He made the bucket carry the water
To wash the floor
Wash the floor
Swish a wish a splash splash
Swish a wish a splash splash
Sweep the floor
Wisk a wisk
Scrub the floor
Scrub a rub
Wash the floor
Swish a wish
He could not stop the long broom sweeping
Brush a brush a wisk wisk,
He could not stop the brush a scrubbing
Scrub a rub scrub a rub,
He could not stop the bucket splashing
Swish a wish a splash splash.
He made the big black kettle boil

Bubble a dubble, bubble a dubble,
He made the big doors open and shut
Slam a bang, slam a bang
Slammity bangity bang bang,
He made the lights switch on and off
A switch a flash, a switch a flash.
He could not stop the kettle boiling
Bubble a dubble, bubble a dubble,
He could not stop the big doors banging
Slam a bang, slam a bang,
He could not stop the lights from flashing
A switch a flash, a switch a flash
A bubble a dubble
Switch a flash
Scrubbity scrub
Splash a splash
Slam a bang
A bang
A bang
Brush a brush a wisk
Bubble a dubble
Switch a flash
Scrubbity scrub
Splash a splash
Slam abang
A bang
A bang
Brush a brush a wisk
The Sorcerer appeared upon the stair;
He wrung his hands,
He tore his hair,
With outstretched hands
And terrible scream

He turned the lad
To a jug of cream.
And the broom stopped sweeping
Brush a brush
The brush stopped scrubbing
Scrub a scrub
The bucket stopped carrying
Splash a splash
The kettle stopped boiling
Bubble a dubble
The doors stopped slamming
Slam a bang
The lights stopped switching
Switch a switch
And on the sorcerer's mat
All that could be seen
Was a big black cat
and A JUG OF CREAM.

Hey-how for Hallowe'en!

Anon

Hey-how for Hallowe'en!
A' the witches tae be seen,
Some black, an' some green,
Hey-how for Hallowe'en,

Queen Nefertiti

Anon

Spin a coin, spin a coin,
   All fall down;
Queen Nefertiti
   Stalks through the town.

Over the pavements
   Her feet go clack,
Her legs are as tall
   As a chimney stack;

Her fingers flicker
   Like snakes in the air,
The walls split open
   At her green-eyed stare;

Her voice is thin
   As the ghosts of bees;
She will crumble your bones,
   She will make your blood freeze.

Spin a coin, spin a coin
   All fall down;
Queen Nefertiti
   Stalks through the town.

Prince Kano

Edward Lowbury

In a dark wood Prince Kano lost his way
And searched in vain through the long summer's day.
At last, when night was near, he came in sight
Of a small clearing filled with yellow light,
And there, bending beside his brazier, stood
A charcoal burner wearing a black hood.
The Prince cried out for joy: "Good friend, I'll give
What you will ask: guide me to where I live."
The man pulled back his hood: he had no face –
Where it should be there was an empty space.

Half dead with fear the Prince staggered away,
Rushed blindly through the wood till break of day;
And then he saw a larger clearing, filled
With houses, people; but his soul was chilled,
He looked around for comfort, and his search
Led him inside a small, half-empty church
Where monks prayed. "Father," to one he said,
"I've seen a dreadful thing; I am afraid."
"What did you see, my son?" "I saw a man
Whose face was like . . . " and, as the prince began,
The monk drew back his hood and seemed to hiss,
Pointing to where his face should be, "Like this?"

Eight Magpies

Anon

I saw eight magpies in a tree,
Two for you and six for me:
One for sorrow, two for mirth,
Three for a wedding, four for a birth,
Five for England, six for France,
Seven for a fiddler, eight for a dance.

The Making of a Charm

From Macbeth

William Shakespeare

Double, double toil and trouble;
Fire, burn; and, cauldron, bubble.

Fillet of a fenny snake,
In the cauldron boil and bake;
Eye of newt, and toe of frog,
Wool of bat, and tongue of dog,
Adder's fork, and blind-worm's sting,
Lizard's leg, and howlet's wing,
For a charm of powerful trouble,
Like a hell-broth boil and bubble.

Double, double toil and trouble;
Fire, burn; and, cauldron, bubble.

The Dragon of Wantley

English folk song

This dragon had two furious wings
One upon each shoulder,
With a sting in his tail as long as a flail
Which made him bolder and bolder.
He had long claws, and in his jaws
Four and forty teeth of iron,
With a hide as tough as any buff
Which did him round environ.

Have you not heard how the Trojan horse
Had seventy men in his belly?
This dragon wasn't quite so big
But very near I'll tell ye.
Devoured he poor children three
That could not with him grapple,
And at one sup he ate them up
As you would eat an apple.

All sorts of cattle this dragon did eat
Some say he ate up trees,
And that the forests sure he would
Devour by degrees.
For houses and churches were to him
   geese and turkeys
He ate all, and left none behind
But some stones, good sirs, that he
   couldn't crack
Which on the hills you'll find.

The Derby Ram

English folk song

As I went down to Derby, sirs,
   all on a market day,
I met the finest ram, sir,
   that ever was fed on hay.

Sing joram, sing joram,
   sing joram dandelay,
I met the finest ram, sir,
   that ever was fed on hay.

He had so large a hoof, sir,
   a hoof so large and round,
That when he put it down, sir,
   it covered an acre of ground.

Sing joram, sing joram,
   Sing joram dandelay,
I met the finest ram, sir,
   that ever was fed on hay.

The wool upon his back, sir,
   reached up into the sky.
The eagles built their nest there,
   I heard the young ones cry.

Sing joram, sing joram,
   Sing joram dandelay,
I met the finest ram, sir,
   that ever was fed on hay.

The horns upon this ram, sir,
    they reached up to the moon.
A man went up in December, sir,
    and didn't come down till June.

The Giant Follderowe

Leslie Norris

Who uses a mountain as his bed
and on the soft clouds rests his head
and never feels he's fully fed?
                The Giant Follderowe.
Whose feet are cold, and white as rice,
who dipped them in the ocean twice
and made the North and South Poles ice?
                The Giant Follderowe.
Whose hand can hide the noonday sun
and make you think that night has come,
whose age is a thousand and ninety-one?
                The Giant Follderowe.
Who's sleeping near the frozen lakes,
snoring and rumbling until the earth shakes?
what's going to happen when he awakes,
                The Giant Follderowe?

The Dragon with a Big Nose

Kathy Henderson

The dragon
with a big nose
and twelve toes
on each foot
eats flies
and mince pies

and sometimes
when he's very bad
whole towns
upside down

streets and houses
shops and churches
schools and factories
undergrounds

swallows them all
quite whole
and spits out the glass fast
treading very carefully
somewhere else
going away.

No one's ever seen him coming
they can't see him leave.
No one's ever seen him anyway
. . . . except me!

What has happened to Lulu?

Charles Causley

What has happened to Lulu, mother?
    What has happened to Lu?
There's nothing in her bed but an old rag-doll
    And by its side a shoe.

Why is her window wide, mother?
    The curtain flapping free,
And only a circle on the dusty shelf
    Where her money-box used to be?

Why do you turn your head, mother,
    And why do the tear-drops fall?
And why do you crumple that note on the fire
    And say it is nothing at all?

I woke to voices late last night,
    I heard an engine roar.
Why do you tell me the things I heard
    Were a dream and nothing more?

I heard somebody cry, mother,
    In anger or in pain,
But now I ask you why, mother,
    You say it was a gust of rain.

Why do you wander about as though
    You don't know what to do?
What has happened to Lulu, mother?
    What has happened to Lu?

Willie Wet-eye

Leslie Norris

The Giant Willie Wet-eye is twenty metres tall,
But he can't climb a tree and he can't throw a ball,
And nobody will play with him, nobody at all.
   Wipe your eyes, Willie, wipe away your tears.

His old uncle Thundervoice is grumbling aloud,
His fierce aunt Wintercold is black as a cloud,
They aren't proud of Willie, not at all proud.
   Wipe your eyes, Willie, wipe away your tears.

His grandfather, old Mountainous, ate twenty men for tea,
His Mother's cousin Blottingpad, drank half the Irish Sea,
But wailing Willie Wet-Eye is afraid of you and me.
   Wipe your eyes, Willie, wipe away your tears.

His mother feeds him oatmeal out of a wooden tub,
His father worries over him and gives his head a rub,
But poor Willie Wet-Eye, all he can do is blub.
   Wipe your eyes, Willie, wipe away your tears.

When the summer comes again we'll call at Willie's
          house,
And talk to him and smile at him and let him play with us,
Poor Willie Wet-Eye, as timid as a mouse.
   Wipe your eyes, Willie, wipe away your tears.

The Tom-cat

Don Marquis

At midnight in the alley
A Tom-cat comes to wail,
And he chants the hate of a million years
As he swings his snaky tail.

Malevolent, bony, brindled,
Tiger and devil and bard,
His eyes are coals from the middle of Hell,
And his heart is black and hard.

He twists and crouches and capers
And bares his curved sharp claws,
And he sings to the stars of the jungle nights,
Ere cities were, or laws.

Beasts from a world primeval,
He and his leaping clan,
When the blotched red moon leers over the roofs,
Give voice to their scorn of man.

He will lie on a rug tomorrow
And lick his silky fur,
And veil the brute in his yellow eyes
And play he's tame, and purr.

But at midnight in the alley
He will crouch again and wail,
And beat the time for his demon's song
With the swing of his demon's tail.

I dreamt I caught a little owl

Christina Rossetti

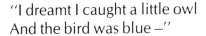

"I dreamt I caught a little owl
And the bird was blue –"

"But you may hunt forever
And not find such a one."

"I dreamt I set a sunflower
And red as blood it grew –"

"But such a sunflower never
Bloomed beneath the sun."

Escape at Bedtime

Robert Louis Stevenson

The lights from the parlour and kitchen shone out
    Through the blinds and the windows and bars;
And high overhead and all moving about,
    There were thousands of millions of stars.
There ne'er were such thousands of leaves on a tree,
    Nor of people in church or the park,
As the crowds of the stars that looked down upon me,
    And that glittered and winked in the dark.
The Dog, and the Plough, and the Hunter, and all,
    And the star of the sailor, and Mars.
These shone in the sky, and the pail by the wall
    Would be half full of water and stars.
They saw me at last, and they chased me with cries,
    And they soon had me packed into bed;
But the glory kept shining and bright in my eyes,
    And the stars going round in my head.

Buses

Michael Rosen

Late last night
I lay in bed,
driving buses
in my head.

My Dream

Anon

I dreamed a dream next Tuesday week,
    Beneath the apple-trees;
I thought my eyes were big pork-pies,
    And my nose was Stilton cheese.
The clock struck twenty minutes to six,
    When a frog sat on my knee;
I asked him to lend me eighteenpence
    But he borrowed tenpence of me.

In Bed

Charlotte Zolotow

When I am in bed
I hear
footsteps of the night
sharp
like the crackling of a dead leaf
in the stillness.

Then my mother laughs
downstairs.

Things that go ''bump'' in the night

Spike Milligan

Things that go ''bump!'' in the night,
Should not really give one a fright.
It's the hole in each ear
That lets in the fear,
That, and the absence of light!

City Lights

Margaret Greaves

Huge round oranges of light
Ripen against the thin dark of the city sky,
Spilling their juice in warm pools
　　on bare dry pavements.
Below them blink the traffic lights
　　like the eyes of enormous cats
Crouching in the dark –
Crouching and breathing with the heavy purr of the traffic;
And winking tail lights slide and dart
　　like goldfish
In the pale streams pouring from
　　shop windows.

Street at night

Thomas Young

Not a sound came from the street
Just some silently stepping feet
Going farther and farther
Growing fainter and fainter
Till they had gone in the distance
and could be heard no more.

The moon

Robert Louis Stevenson

The moon has a face like the clock in the hall;
She shines on thieves on the garden wall,
On streets and fields and harbour quays,
And birdies asleep in the forks of the trees.

The squalling cat and the squeaking mouse,
The howling dog by the door of the house,
The bat that lies in bed at noon,
All love to be out by the light of the moon.

But all of the things that belong to the day
Cuddle to sleep to be out of her way;
And flowers and children close their eyes,
Till up in the morning the sun shall arise.

From The Moon

Emily Dickinson

The moon was but a chin of gold
A night or two ago,
And now she turns her perfect face
Upon the world below.

The Song of the Stars

From a Pasamaquoddy Indian song

We are the stars which sing.
We sing with our light.
We are the birds of fire.
We fly across the heaven.

The Falling Star

Sara Teasdale

I saw a star slide down the sky,
Blinding the north as it went by,
Too burning and too quick to hold,
Too lovely to be bought or sold,
Good only to make wishes on
And then forever to be gone.

The Night Sky

Anon

All day long
   The sun shines bright.
The moon and stars
   Come out by night.
From twilight time
   They line the skies
And watch the world
   With quiet eyes.

The Night Will Never Stay

Eleanor Farjeon

The night will never stay,
The night will still go by,
Though with a million stars
You pin it to the sky;
Though you bind it with the blowing wind
And buckle it with the moon,
The night will slip away
Like sorrow or a tune.

Stopping by Woods on a Snowy Evening

Robert Frost

Whose woods these are I think I know.
His house is in the village though;
He will not see me stopping here
To watch his woods fill up with snow.

My little horse must think it queer
To stop without a farmhouse near
Between the woods and frozen lake,
The darkest evening of the year.

He gives his harness bells a shake
To ask if there is some mistake.
The only other sound's the sweep
Of easy wind and downy flake.

The woods are lovely, dark and deep,
But I have promises to keep,
And miles to go before I sleep,
And miles to go before I sleep.

Home

Leonard Clark

Snow in the air tonight,
Roads freeze:
No birds sing, cold trees,
But the kitchen is warm, bright.

Check

James Stephens

The Night was creeping on the ground;
She crept and did not make a sound
Until she reached the tree, and then
She covered it, and stole again
Along the grass beside the wall.

I heard the rustle of her shawl
As she threw blackness everywhere
Upon the sky and ground and air,
And in the room where I was hid:
But no matter what she did
To everything that was without,
She could not put my candle out.

So I stared at the night, and she
Stared back solemnly at me.

The Silent Spinney

Seamus Redmond

What's that rustling behind me?
Only a cat.
Thank goodness for that,
For I'm afraid of the darkness,
And these tall trees
Are silent and black,
And if I ever get out of here, mate,
I can tell you I'm not coming back.

There's a dark shadow out in the roadway;
See if there's someone behind that tree,
For I'm afraid of the darkness
And it might jump out at me.

My sisters are scared stiff of spiders,
My mother is frightened of mice,
But I'm afraid of the darkness,
I'm not coming this way twice.

The Witch's Cat

Ian Serraillier

"My magic is dead," said the witch. "I'm astounded
That people can fly to the moon and around it.
It used to be mine and the cat's till they found it.
My broomstick is draughty, I snivel with cold
As I ride to the stars. I'm painfully old,
 And so is my cat;
 But planet-and-space-ship
 Rocket or race-ship
Never shall part me from that."

She wrote an advertisement. "Witch in a fix
Willing to part with the whole bag of tricks,
Going cheap at the price at eighteen and six."
But no-one was ready to empty his coffers
For out of date rubbish. There weren't any offers—
 Except for the cat.
 "But planet-and-space-ship
 Rocket or race-ship
Never shall part me from that."

The tears trickled fast, not a sentence she spoke
As she stamped on her broom and the brittle stick broke,
And she dumped in a dustbin her hat and her cloak,
Then clean disappeared, leaving no prints;
And no one at all has set eyes on her since
 Or her tired old cat.
 "But planet-and-space-ship,
 Rocket or race-ship
Never shall part me from that."

if you can't eat you got to

e e cummings

if you can't eat you got to

smoke and we aint got
nothing to smoke: come on kid

let's go to sleep
if you can't smoke you got to

Sing and we aint got

nothing to sing; come on kid
let's go to sleep

if you can't sing you got to
die and we aint got

Nothing to die, come on kid

let's go to sleep
if you can't die you got to

dream and we aint got
nothing to dream (come on kid

Let's go to sleep)

Tom Cat Fight

Kathryn Lister (10)

I was wakened from my sleep one night
By a noise that made me shiver with fright.
Like the echo of a ghostly cry,
Like the scream of a witch as she went by,
Like the wailing of someone in terrible pain,
It stopped, then pierced the night again.
Someone opened their window and began to shout,
"Get away you cats – go on, get out!"
Then I knew that the terrible noise in the night
Was the wailing and shrieking of a tom-cat fight.

Dreams

J Charles

What did you dream of last night?
Dolls and toys and joys so bright,
and blossoming trees.

What are you dreaming tonight?
Of love and marriage and delight,
and leafy trees.

What will you dream of tomorrow?
Wrinkles and loneliness and sorrow,
and leafless trees.

From At Night in the Wood

Nancy M Hayes

The Stoat, the Rat
And the squeaking Bat
All open their keen little eyes
And rise.
And the Hedgehog peeps from his cosy nest
And hurries out with the rest.
The bark of the Fox shows he's astir,
And the Rabbit shivers within his fur.

Mystery Planet

Margaret (11)

When they get out of the space ship
Every thing is beautiful to behold,
There are golden flowers, blue grass and happy trees
Which bend down to give you fruit and drink.
The sun shines brighter than on earth
The air is dazzling and clear like lemonade,
And everyone is happy like the garden of Eden.
There are little animals dancing about
Lions and tigers playing with the children
And no-one comes to any harm,
For everything is wonderful.

Space Poem

John Mills

In the velvet blue blackness
Millions of stars appear,
Moving in set order with their trailing moons.
We are more minute than a microscopic creature
       against the vastness of this galaxy.
Man's future mind
Makes vehicles to conquer the immensity of Space
For what?
Man's home is here.

Mars

Anon

And then in my dream I slipped away
To the silver ship in the dawn of day,
To the grasshopper men with their queer green eyes
And suits that glittered in splendid dyes.
They came, they said, from a thirsty land,
A land that was dead and choked with sand;
The wells were empty and dusty and dry,
And the burning sun hung low in the sky;
"We are old," they said. "We have had our day,
And the silent cities crumble away."
"Yet here," they said, "we may find again
All that was carefree and lovely then
When the wells were full and the cities rang
With the harvest song that the reapers sang!"

. . . . .

Oh, when I'm a man I shall travel to Mars
In a silver ship, in a night of stars,
And there I shall see those grasshopper men.
Without any doubt I shall know them again.

A Space Odyssey

Adrian Rumble

Heart in my mouth
the countdown starts.
Years of preparation
tick off in seconds.
Ignition!
Our ship roars,
rumbles,
stutters.
Shuddering,
shaking, juddering,
we rise!
Slow and ponderous,
a great reluctant elephant.
Rising,
rising higher.
A flaming eruption
tugging against the
pull of the world.
Higher,
swifter,
straighter –
an arrow
from a bow.
We hit
the blue and
leave the world behind.

Burning, burning moonward
straight across the sky
deep into the universe
toward the moon on high.

Behind us now in blackness –
Earth misty white and blue,
lovely and abandoned,
breathless bright and new.

Gliding, gliding moonward,
dancing though a void
turning to the music
of star and asteroid.

Gigantic looming satellite,
pocked and cratered crust,
silver ashen-grey,
cold rock and ancient dust.

Falling, falling moonward,
heart pounding in my chest,
hiss of retro-fire,
and our space-craft comes to rest.

3

The airlock swings open –
behold! a new world.
Obsidian black sky
lit by the sun's
fierce glare.

Inch
down the ladder —
the first man on the moon!
Look! the first footprint.
Listen! the first word
splitting the still, dead silence.
Dead dust
dead rock
dead black sky.
A dead, dead world.
Zombie in a moontrance I
trip
stumble
fall
rise
before the slow dust settles.
I leap in lingering arches . . .
Steady yourself,
get your samples —
moondust
moonrock.
Temperature check.
Humidity test.

And so
plod
carefully back.
My footprints in the ancient dust

4

Module calling earth –
tell me do you read?
Our mission's been completed
and you never would believe –
there's a new earth on the rise!

Module calling earth –
tell me do you read?
We've made it. Yes, we've made it
and you never would believe –
there's a new earth on the rise!

We're on our way back home
so tell them all from Peking through to Rome
they can all stay up and watch us on T.V.
And you never would believe –
there's a new earth on the rise!

There's a new earth on the rise!
Yes, a good earth on the rise,
a blue earth and a green earth,
a fresh earth and a clean earth.
Tell me – could we please keep it that way?

Night Clouds

Amy Lowell

The white mares of the moon rush along the sky
Beating their golden hoofs upon the glass Heavens;
The white mares of the moon are all standing on their hind
        legs
Pawing at the green porcelain doors of the remote
        Heavens.
Fly, mares!
Strain your utmost,
Scatter the milky dust of stars,
Or the tiger sun will leap upon you and destroy you
With one lick of his vermilion tongue.

MY MOTHER SAW A DANCING BEAR

From The History of the Flood

John Heath-Stubbs

Bang Bang Bang
Said the nails in the Ark.

It's getting rather dark
Said the nails in the Ark.

For the rain is coming down
Said the nails in the Ark.

And you're all like to drown
Said the nails in the Ark.

Dark and black as sin
Said the nails in the Ark.

So won't you all come in
Said the nails in the Ark.

But only two by two
Said the nails in the Ark.

So they came in two by two,
The elephant, the kangaroo,
And the gnu,
And the little tiny shrew.

Then the birds
Flocked in like wingèd words:
Two racket-tailed motmots, two macaws,
Two nuthatches and two
Little bright robins.

And the reptiles: the gila monster, the slow-worm,
The green mamba, the cotton mouth, and the alligator –
All squirmed in;
And after a very lengthy walk,
Two giant Galapagos tortoises.

And the insects in their hierarchies:
A queen ant, a king ant, a queen wasp, a king wasp,
A queen bee, a king bee,
And all the beetles, bugs and mosquitoes,
Cascaded in like glittering, murmurous jewels.

          . . . . .

God put a rainbow in the sky.
They wondered what it was for.
There had never been a rainbow before.
The rainbow was a sign;
It looked like a neon sign –
Seven colours arched in the skies:
What should it publicize?
They looked up with wondering eyes.

It advertises Mercy
Said the nails in the Ark.

Mercy Mercy Mercy
Said the nails in the Ark.

Our God is merciful
Said the nails in the Ark

Merciful and gracious
Bang Bang Bang Bang.

The Signifying Monkey

Traditional American

The Monkey and the Lion
Got to talking one day.
Monkey looked down and said, "Lion,
I hear you're king in every way.
But I know somebody
Who does not think that is true —
He told me he could whip
The living daylights out of you."
Lion said, "Who?"
Monkey said, "Lion,
He talked about your mama
And talked about your grandma, too.
And I'm too polite to tell you
What he said about you."
Lion said, "Who said what? Who?"
Monkey in the tree,
Lion on the ground.
Monkey kept on signifying
But he didn't come down.
Monkey said, "His name is Elephant —
He stone sure is not your friend."
Lion said, "He don't need to be
Because today will be his end."
Lion took off through the jungle
Lickity-split,
Meaning to grab Elephant
And tear him bit to bit. Full stop!
He came across Elephant copping a righteous nod
Under a fine cool shady tree.

Lion said, "You big old no-good so-and-so,
It's either you or me."
Lion let out a solid roar
And bopped Elephant with his paw.
Elephant just took his trunk
and busted old Lion's jaw.
Lion let out another roar,
Reared up six feet tall.
Elephant just kicked him in the belly
And laughed to see him drop and fall.
Lion rolled over,
Copped Elephant by the throat.
Elephant just shook him loose
And butted him like a goat,
Then he tromped him and he stomped him
Till the Lion yelled, "Oh, no!"
And it was nigh near sunset
When Elephant let Lion go.
The signifying Monkey
Was still sitting in his tree
When he looked down and saw the Lion.
Said, "Why Lion who can that there be?"
Lion said, "Monkey, I don't want
To hear your jive-end jive."
Monkey just kept on signifying,
"Lion, you for sure caught hell –
Mister Elephant's whipped you
To a fare-thee-well!
You ain't no king to me.
Fact is, I don't think that you
Can even as much as roar –
And if you try I'm liable
To come down out of this tree and
Whip your tail some more."

The Monkey started laughing
And jumping up and down.
But he jumped so hard the limb broke
And he landed – bam! – on the ground.
When he went to run, his foot slipped
And he fell flat down.
Grr-rrr-rr-r! The Lion was on him
With his front feet and his hind.
Monkey hollered, "Ow!
I didn't mean it, Mister Lion!"
Lion said, "You little flea bag you!
Why, I'll eat you up alive.
I wouldn't a-been in this fix at all
Wasn't for your signifying jive."
"*Please*," said Monkey, "Mister Lion,
If you'll just let me go,
I got something to tell you, please,
I think you ought to know."
Lion let the Monkey loose
To see what his tale would be –
And Monkey jumped right back on up
Into his tree.
"What I was gonna tell you," said Monkey,
"Is, you square old so-and-so,
If you fool with me I'll get
Elephant to whip your head some more."
"Monkey," said the Lion,
Beat to his unbooted knees,
"You and all your signifying children
Better stay up in them trees."
Which is why today
Monkey does his signifying
A-way-up out of the way.

Mole

Alan Brownjohn

To have to be a mole?

It is like, in a way,
being a little car driven
in the very dark,
                    owned
by these endless-
ly tunnelling paws and small
eyes that are good, only,
for the underground.

What can you know of me, this
warm black engine of
busying velvet?

Soft mounds of new, pale
earth like finely-flaked ash
tell you just about where

my country is, but
do you ever see
                    me?

From Centipedes Song

Roald Dahl

"I've eaten many strange and scrumptious dishes in my
     time,
Like jellied gnats and dandyprats and earwigs cooked in
     slime,
And mice with rice – they're really nice
When roasted in their prime.
(But don't forget to sprinkle them with just a pinch of
     grime.)

"I've eaten fresh mudburgers by the greatest cooks there
     are,
And scrambled dregs and stinkbug's eggs and hornets
     stewed in tar,
And pails of snails and lizards' tails,
And beetles by the jar.
(A beetle is improved by just a splash of vinegar.)

"I often eat boiled slobbages. They're grand when served
     beside
Minced doodlebugs and curried slugs. And have you ever
     tried
Mosquitoes' toes and wampfish roes
Most delicately fried?
(The only trouble is they disagree with my inside.)

"I'm mad for crispy wasp-stings on a piece of buttered
     toast,
And pickled spines of porcupines. And then a gorgeous
     roast
Of dragon's flesh, well hung, not fresh –
It costs a pound at most,

(And comes to you in barrels if your order it by post.)

"I crave the tasty tentacles of octopi for tea.
I like hot-dogs, I LOVE hot-frogs, and surely you'll agree
A plate of soil with engine oil's
A super recipe.
(I hardly need to mention that it's practically free.)

"For dinner on my birthday shall I tell you what I chose:
Hot noodles made from poodles on a slice of garden hose –
And a rather smelly jelly
Made of armadillo's toes.
(The jelly is delicious, but you have to hold your nose.")

The Spider

John Clare

The mottled spider, at eve's leisure, weaves
His webs of silken lace on twigs and leaves,
Which every morning meets the poet's eye,
Like fairies' dew-wet tresses hung to dry.

The Bat

Theodore Roethke

By day the bat is cousin to the mouse.
He likes the attic of an ageing house.

His fingers make a hat about his head.
His pulse beat is so slow we think him dead.

He loops in crazy figures half the night
Among the trees that face the corner light.

But when he brushes up against a screen,
We are afraid of what our eyes have seen:

For something is amiss or out of place
When mice with wings can wear a human face.

Black dot

Libby Houston

a black dot
a jelly tot

a water-wriggler
a tail jiggler

a leg-kicker
a sitting slicker

a panting puffer
a fly-snuffer

a high-hopper
a belly-flopper

a catalogue
     to make me

       FROG

Boy and Fish

Leonard Clark

The sun is bright and clear, fish.
                    Thank you, we can see it, boy.
The sand is soft and warm, fish.
                    We don't care a bit, boy.
My feet are making rings, fish.
                    We can make them, too, boy.
I'm looking hard at you, fish.
                    We're looking hard at you, boy.
I have a little net, fish.
                    So that's your little plan, boy.
I'm going to catch you now, fish.
                    Well, catch us if you can, boy.
I have my bucket here, fish.
                    Then fill it to the top, boy.
There's room for all of you, fish.
                    We really cannot stop, boy.
Tomorrow I'll be back, fish.
                    Tomorrow we'll be here, boy.
I'll have another try, fish.
                    The sun is bright and clear, boy.

To a squirrel at Kyle-na-no

W B Yeats

Come play with me;
Why should you run
Through the shaking tree
As though I'd a gun
To strike you dead?
When all I would do
Is to scratch your head
And let you go.

Squirrel

John Buxton

I saw a squirrel
Run through the wood.
By every tree
It stopped; and stood
Ready to climb,
With its paws on the trunk,
And every time
(For no danger came)
It hurried on,
And was gone.

The Mouse in the Wainscot

Ian Serraillier

Hush, Suzanne!
Don't lift your cup.
That breath you heard
Is a mouse getting up.

As the mist that steams
From your milk as you sup,
So soft is the sound
Of a mouse getting up.

There! Did you hear
His feet pitter-patter,
Lighter than tipping
Of beads in a platter,

And then like a shower
On the window pane
The little feet scampering
Back again?

O falling of feather!
O drift of a leaf!
The mouse in the wainscot
Is dropping asleep.

Anne and the Field-mouse

Ian Serraillier

We found a mouse in the chalk quarry today
In a circle of stones and empty oil drums
By the fag ends of a fire. There had been
A picnic there; he must have been after the crumbs.

Jane saw him first, a flicker of brown fur
In and out of the charred wood and chalk-white.
I saw him last, but not till we'd turned up
Every stone and surprised him into flight.

Though not far – little zig-zag spurts from stone
To stone. Once, as he lurked in his hiding-place
I saw his beady eyes uplifted to mine.
I'd never seen such terror in so small a face.

I watched, amazed and guilty. Beside us suddenly
A heavy pheasant whirred up from the ground,
Scaring us all; and, before we knew it, the mouse
Had broken cover, skimming away without a sound.

Melting into the nettles. We didn't go
Till I'd chalked in capitals on a rusty can:
THERE'S A MOUSE IN THOSE NETTLES. LEAVE
HIM ALONE. NOVEMBER 15TH. ANNE.

The Kangaroo

Traditional Australian

Old Jumpety-Bumpety-Hop-and-Go-One
Was lying asleep on his side in the sun.
This old Kangaroo, he was whisking the flies
(With his long glossy tail) from his ears and his eyes.
Jumpety-Bumpety-Hop-and-Go-One
Was lying asleep on his side in the sun,
Jumpety-Bumpety-Hop!

My Mother Saw a Dancing Bear

Charles Causley

My mother saw a dancing bear
By the schoolyard, a day in June.
The keeper stood with chain and bar
And whistle-pipe, and played a tune.

And bruin lifted up its head
And lifted up its dusty feet,
And all the children laughed to see
It caper in the summer heat.

They watched as for the Queen it died.
They watched it march. They watched it halt.
They heard the keeper as he cried,
"Now, roly-poly!" "Somersault!"

And then, my mother said, there came
The keeper with a begging-cup.
The bear with burning coat of fur,
Shaming the laughter to a stop.

They paid a penny for the dance,
But what they saw was not the show;
Only, in Bruin's aching eyes,
Far-distant forests, and the snow.

Miss Tuckett

Anon

Little Miss Tuckett
Sat on a bucket,
Eating some peaches and cream;
There came a grasshopper
And tried hard to stop her;
But she said, "Go away, or I'll scream".

The Wasp

William Sharp

Where the ripe pears droop heavily,
The yellow wasp hums loud and long
His hot and drowsy autumn song:
A yellow flame he seems to be,
When darting suddenly from high
He lights where fallen peaches lie:

Yellow and black this tiny thing's
A tiger-soul on elfin wings.

Hurt No Living Thing

Christina Rossetti

Hurt no living thing;
Ladybird, nor butterfly,
Nor moth with dusty wing,
Nor cricket chirping cheerily,
Nor grasshopper so light of leap,
Nor dancing gnat, nor beetle fat,
Nor harmless worms that creep.

The Fly

Walter de la Mare

How large unto the tiny fly
  Must little things appear! –
A rosebud like a feather bed,
  Its prickle like a spear;

A dewdrop like a looking-glass,
  A hair like a golden wire;
The smallest grain of mustard-seed
  As fierce as coals of fire;

A loaf of bread, a lofty hill;
  A wasp, a cruel leopard;
And specks of salt as bright to see
  As lambkins to a shepherd.

The cheetah, my dearest, is known not to cheat

George Barker

The cheetah, my dearest, is known not to cheat;
the tiger possesses no tie;
the horse-fly, of course, was never a horse;
the lion will not tell a lie.

The turkey, though perky, was never a Turk;
nor the monkey ever a monk;
the mandrel, though like one, was never a man,
but some men are like him, when drunk.

The springbok, dear thing, was not born in the Spring;
the walrus will not build a wall.
No badger is bad; no adder can add.
There is no truth in these things at all.

Puma

George Barker

Within the Puma's golden head
   burn Jungle, flames and paradises.
And all who look into his red
and fiery eye by fury fed
   the Puma paralyses.

The Sun, the Orchid, and the Snake
   like demons of the Bible
rage in his brow. The earthquake
and the volcanic mountain shake
   and tremble in his eyeball.

Rattlesnake

Traditional American

Rattlesnake, O rattlesnake,
What makes your teeth so white?
I've been in the bottom all my life,
An' I ain't done nothin' but bite, bite,
Ain't done nothin' but bite.

Muskrat, O muskrat,
What makes you smell so bad?
I've been in the bottom all of my life
Till I'm mortified in my head, head,
I'm mortified in my head.

Groundhog, groundhog,
What makes your back so brown?
It's a wonder I don't smotherfy,
Livin' down in the ground, ground,
Livin' down in the ground.

Rooster, O rooster,
What makes your claws so hard?
Been scratchin' this gravel all my days,
It's a wonder I ain't tired, tired,
It's a wonder I ain't tired.

Jaybird, O jaybird,
What makes you fly so high?
Been robbin' your cornpatch all my life,
It's a wonder I don't die, die,
It's a wonder I don't die.

Snake

George Barker

I, the reptilian,
Serpentine, jewel-eyed,
golden-scaled, spiralling
splendour of Snake,
I in the shallows of
Nigers and Amazons
I dream of Death
when I sleep, when I wake.
I bind the Bird and
the Beast and
all creatures in
my coiled fascination
no Lion could break.

I am the Python,
the Great Anaconda,
I am the Cobra the
King of Golconda,
I am the Winged, the
Plumed Aztec Serpent.

I am the Rainbow
that climbs in the tree,
I am the Kiss of Death,
the hiss of Darkness,
I and I only
do not fear me.

Curiosity

Adrian Rumble

A hedgehog came into our garden today,
Grunting and snuffling and shuffling his way
To where our mother was hanging the washing to dry,
In the cold, grey, late November.
Hardly more than a baby, his spikes scarcely stiff;
Two black button eyes; wet, curious snout.
He didn't curl up; he didn't run away –
Perhaps HIS mother wasn't too far away – and felt
Safe enough to let my sister and I
Touch his bristly coat carefully,
Just in case.
We laughed, and we shouted, "Look Mummy! Look
            Mummy!"
But, before she could turn, he gave
A twitch of his nose, and trotted back
To his mother in the bushes.

From Reynard the Fox

John Masefield

The fox was strong, he was full of running,
He could run for an hour and then be cunning,
But the cry behind him made him chill,
They were nearer now and they meant to kill.
They meant to run him until his blood
Clogged on his heart as his brush with mud,
Till his back bent up and his tongue hung flagging,
And his belly and brush were filthed from dragging.

. . . . .

As he raced the corn towards Wan Dyke Brook
The pack had view of the way he took;
The quarter mile to the Wan Brook's brink
Was raced as quick as a man can think.

. . . . .

He raced the trench, past the rabbit warren,
Close-grown with moss which the wind made barren;
He passed the spring where the rushes spread,
And there in the stones was his earth ahead.
One last short burst upon failing feet –
There life lay waiting, so sweet, so sweet,
Rest in a darkness, balm for aches.

The earth was stopped. It was barred with stakes.

A fox came into my Garden

Charles Causley

A fox came into my garden.
"What do you want from me?"
"Heigh-ho, Johnnie-boy,
A chicken for my tea."

"Oh no, you beggar, and never, you thief,
My chicken you must leave,
That she may run and she may fly
From now to Christmas Eve."

"What are you eating, Johnnie-boy,
Between two slices of bread?"
"I'm eating a piece of chicken-breast
And it's honey-sweet," I said.

"Heigh-ho, you diddling man,
I thought that was what I could smell.
What, some for you and none for me?
Give us a piece as well!"

The Rabbit

Elizabeth Madox Roberts

When they said the time to hide was mine,
I hid back under a thick grape vine.

And while I was still for the time to pass
A little grey thing came out of the grass.

He hopped his way through the melon bed
And sat down close by a cabbage head.

He sat down close where I could see,
And his big still eyes looked hard at me,

His big eyes bursting out of the rim,
And I looked back very hard at him.

I'm not frightened of Pussy Cats

Spike Milligan

I'm not frightened of Pussy Cats,
They only eat up mice and rats,
But a Hippopotamus
Could eat the Lotofus.

Cats

Eleanor Farjeon

Cats sleep
Anywhere,
Any table,
Any chair,
Top of piano,
Window-ledge,
In the middle,
On the edge,
Open drawer,
Empty shoe,
Anybody's
Lap will do,
Fitted in a
Cardboard box,
In the cupboard
With your frocks —
Anywhere!
They don't care!
Cats sleep
Anywhere.

Rock, Our Dog

Nicholas Hadfield

He's dead now.
He was put to sleep last night.
I was sad,
But I did not cry.

It was not the same
Without him there
To prance and
Muzzle his head
Into my arms.

Today we were going
To bury him
In the garden.
I helped dig the hole,
And then ran off.

Me and my dog

Anon

Me and my dog
have tramped together
in cold weather
and hot.

Me and my dog
don't care whether
we get any work
or not

Porridge

Clive Riche

I didn't like my porridge,
But my mummy made me have it.
So while she wasn't looking,
I gave it to my rabbit.

I gave it to my rabbit,
But he was eating carrots,
He didn't want it either,
So I gave it to my parrot.

But he was busy crunching,
Brown nuts on a big brown log.
He didn't want it either,
So I gave it to my dog.

My dog he had a juicy bone,
He didn't want it either,
So while no one was looking,
I threw it on the fire.

It hissed and steamed and sizzled,
As porridge will when burning.
And then I heard my mummy's feet,
Into the room returning.

She said, "You ate that quickly,
Faster than I ever saw,
You must have really liked it,"
And she dished me out some more.

Take one home for the kiddies

Philip Larkin

On shallow straw, in shadeless glass,
Huddled by empty bowls, they sleep:
No dark, no dam, no earth, no grass –
Mam, get us one of them to keep.

Living toys are something novel,
But it soon wears off somehow.
Fetch the shoe box, fetch the shovel –
Mam, we're playing funerals now.

The Pasture

Robert Frost

I'm going out to clean the pasture spring;
I'll only stop to rake the leaves away
(And wait to watch the water clear, I may):
I shan't be gone long. – You come too.

I'm going out to fetch the little calf
That's standing by the mother. It's so young
It totters when she licks it with her tongue.
I shan't be gone long. – You come too.

Donkeys

Jean Kenward

Trit-trat –
Donkeys' feet
Make a pattern
In the street:
Make a pattern
Make a tune.
Listen!
They'll be coming soon.....
Donkey's breath
Can blow as sweet
As a field
Of marguerite;
Lines of darkness
On their backs,
Hooves as sharp
As carpet tacks,
Steps so delicate
And small
You'd think nobody
At all
Could be elegant
As that –
Trit-trot –
Trat!

Rhyme for a Donkey

Anon

Donkey walks on four legs,
I walk on two;
The last one I saw
Was just like you.

Good Company

Leonard Clark

I sleep in a room at the top of the house
With a flea, and a fly, and a soft-scratching mouse,
And a spider that hangs by a thread from the ceiling,
Who gives me each day such a curious feeling
When I watch him at work on the beautiful weave
Of his web that's so fine I can hardly believe
It won't all end up in such terrible tangles,
For he sways as he weaves, and spins as he dangles.
I cannot get up to that spider, I know,
And I hope he won't get down to me here below,
And yet when I wake in the chill morning air
I'd miss him if he were not still swinging there,
For I have in my room such good company,
There's him, and the mouse, and the fly, and the flea.

Henry Jack

Janet A Smith

There once was a boy called Henry Jack
Who put a worm down his sister's back.
"You're a horrible boy" his sister said,
And she put the worm down Henry's bed.
Henry mad with rage and shock
Put a slug in his sister's sock.
His sister said, "The little pest!"
And put a spider in Henry's vest.
Henry without more ado,
Put a snail in his sister's shoe.
His sister said, "He must be stopped,"
And into Henry's room she popped
A crocodile that with one crunch,
Ate Henry's trousers for his lunch.
So remember what happened to Henry Jack
Before you put a worm down your sister's back!

Money Spider

Donald Mattam

If I stay still,
Don't move at all,
Just let it crawl
And when it will
Go on its way,
The old people say
That because I've been kind
It will leave luck behind,
The sort that jingles
In pockets and purses
And pink piggy-banks.

But how my cheek tingles!
These very small feet
Though they don't hurt at all
Make my skin start to crawl.
Just as *they* do. It's funny …

Oh, keep your old money!

Meeting

From Hedgehog in an Air Raid

Clifford Dyment

Over the grass a hedgehog came
Questing the air for scents of food
And the cracked twig of danger.
He shuffled near in the gloom. Then stopped.
He was aware of me. I went up,
Bent low to look at him, and saw
His coat of lances pointing to my hand.
What could I do
To show I was no enemy?
I turned him over, inspected his small clenched paws,
His eyes expressionless as glass,
And did not know how I could speak,
By tongue, or touch, the language of a friend.

Out of the Ark

From The Flaming Terrapin

Roy Campbell

Out of the Ark's grim hold
A torrent of splendour rolled –
From the hollow resounding sides,
Flashing and glittering, came
Panthers with sparkled hides,
And tigers scribbled with flame,
And lions in grisly trains
Cascading their golden manes.
They ramped in the morning light,
And over their stripes and stars
The sun-shot lightnings, quivering bright,
Rippled in zig-zag bars.

LOAVES OF BLUE HEAVEN

The Crow

Russell Hoban

Flying loose and easy, where does he go
Swaggering in the sky, what does he know,
Why is he laughing, the carrion crow?
Why is he shouting, why won't he sing,
How did he steal them, whom will he bring
Loaves of blue heaven under each wing?

Larks

Katherine Tynan

All day in exquisite air
The song clomb an invisible stair,
Flight on flight, storey on storey,
Into the dazzling glory.

There was no bird, only a singing,
Up in the glory, climbing and ringing,
Like a small golden cloud at even,
Trembling 'twixt earth and heaven.

I saw no staircase, winding, winding,
Up in the dazzle, sapphire and blinding,
Yet round by round, in exquisite air,
The song went up the stair.

The Crushed Egg

Christina Rossetti

Hear what the mournful linnets say:
   "We built our nest compact and warm,
But cruel boys came round our way
   And took our summerhouse by storm.

"They crushed the eggs so neatly laid;
   So now we sit with drooping wing,
And watch the ruin they have made,
   Too late to build, too sad to sing."

To a Skylark

Percy Bysshe Shelley

Higher still and higher,
   From the earth thou springest,
Like a cloud of fire,
   The blue deep thou wingest,
And singing still dost soar, and soaring ever singest.

The Thrush's Nest

John Clare

Within a thick and spreading hawthorn bush,
That overhung a molehill large and round,
I heard from morn to morn a merry thrush
Sing hymns to sunrise, and I drank the sound
With joy; and often, an intruding guest,
I watched her secret toil from day to day
How true she warped the moss, to form a nest,
And modelled it within with wood and clay;
And by and by, like heath bells gilt with dew,
There lay her shining eggs, as bright as flowers,
Ink-spotted, over shells of greeny blue;
And there I witnessed in the sunny hours,
A brood of nature's minstrels chirp and fly,
Glad as the sunshine and the laughing sky.

Little Bird

Charlotte Zolotow

Little hurt bird
in my hand
your heart beats
like the pound of the sea
under the warmth
of your soft feathers.

The Bird of Night

Randall Jarrell

A shadow is floating through the moonlight.
Its wings don't make a sound.
Its claws are long, its beak is bright.
Its eyes try all the corners of the night.

It calls and calls: all the air swells and heaves
And washes up and down like water.
The ear that listens to the owl believes
in death. The bat beneath the eaves,

The mice beside the stone are still as death.
The owl's air washes them like water.
The owl goes back and forth inside the night,
And the night holds its breath.

The Redbreast

Anthony Rye

The redbreast smoulders in the waste of snow:
His eye is large and bright, and to and fro
He draws and draws his slender threads of sound
Between the dark boughs and the freezing ground.

The Owl

Walter de la Mare

Owl of the wildwood I:
Muffled in sleep I drowse,
Where no fierce sun in heaven
Can me arouse.

My haunt's a hollow
In a half-dead tree,
Whose strangling ivy
Shields, and shelters me.

But when dark's starlight
Thrids my green domain,
My plumage trembles and stirs,
I wake again:

A spectral moon
Silvers the world I see;
Out of their daylong lairs
Creep thievishly

Night's living things.
Then I,
Wafted away on soundless pinions
Fly;
Curdling her arches
With my hunting cry:

A – hooh! a hooh:
Four notes; and then,
Solemn, sepulchral, cold,
Four notes again,
The listening dingles
Of my woodland through:
Ahooh! A-hooh!
A-hooh!

The Rook

James Earp (12)

Black as night it cuts through the air,
Its wide wings spread,
Flap and wave.
Scavenger.
Soft of touch,
But as tough as leather.
Oily wings like cast-off rags,
The rook.
A ready beak to tear and rip,
Eyes like coals, cold and dark,
With hoarse cry
And stupid.

Vulture

George Barker

Veering and wheeling
High in the ceiling
Of the Sahara sky
I can tell a bone
from a whitewashed stone
with my telescopic eye.

I look like a witch
flown up out of a ditch
dishevelled and dirty but never-
the-less horrifying,
for I eat the dying
and dead who are with me for ever.

My hooked beak is like
a scythe or a spike
for tearing the flesh from the skeleton.
My skin is as hoary
as the Old Hermit's story
or the filthy old paper they tell it on.

I love offal and scrag
or a bit of old rag
and for sweets I eat eyeballs of camels;
the most delicious
of edible dishes
for me is the dead flesh of mammals.

Vulture on high
I watch heroes die
as they fail to traverse the Sahara;
I drop like a wreath
on their bones underneath,
then I place their false teeth
on my bald head like a tiara.

The Red Cockatoo

Arthur Waley

Sent as a present from Annam –
A red cockatoo.
Coloured like the peach-tree blossom,
Speaking with the speech of men.
And they did to it what is always done
To the learned and eloquent.
They took a cage with stout bars
And shut it up inside.

Magpie in the Snow

Michael Tanner

White land
Black veins of branches
Dead blue eye of the sky
Magpie flicks tail
Dances
Winks a living eye.

East wind
Dry bones of branches
Scoured and aching sky
Magpie cocks head
Listens
Views the world awry.

Hard ground
Thin roof of branches
Far unfriendly sky
Magpie cares naught
Chatters
Flings its wings to fly.

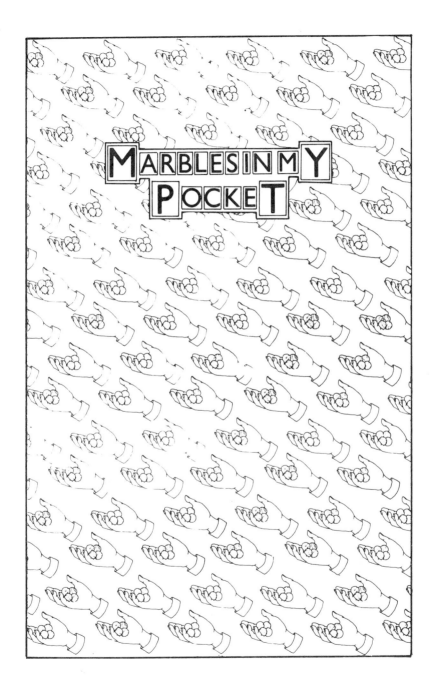

At the Bus Stop

Margaret Holmes

Ten are queueing in the rain.
One decides to go by train.
Nine are waiting – drenched and late
Taxi stops and now there're eight
Still they stay. "Where IS eleven?"
One walks off and now there're seven
Grumpy. Tense. They start to curse.
One jumps on a passing hearse.
Now the six united wail
Then impatient, one turns tail.
Five infuriated folk
Cough and sneeze and wheeze and croak
"I can't stand this any more,"
Someone cries, and now there're four.
Sports car stops with shiny bonnet
"Right. Here goes," and one lands on it.
Three are left, bereft and glum
Praying that the bus will come.
One despairing, thumbs a ride.
Only two remain outside.
"Coffee?" "What a good idea!"
He and she then disappear.

"Drive on Charlie." "No queue." "Strange."
"Well I guess it makes a change!"

My best friend Josephine James

Janet A Smith

My best friend Josephine James
Has called me horrible names.
I know that it's true
Because she told Betty Drew
Who told Ermintrude Jones
Who told Mildred Magrew
Who told Fatima Pugh
Who told ME
That Josephine called me some names.

Oh, I'm cross with Josephine James
So I shall call HER some names,
Like Freckly Frump
Grumbly Grump
Or Lumpetty Lump
Or Silly Old Chump!
Can YOU think of horrible names
For my best friend Josephine James?

The Other Side of the Pancake

Adrian Rumble

O.K. So I made a fatal mistake.
But – what would you have done
in my place?
I mean, there I was,
in the frying pan,
getting hotter and hotter
and it hurt I can tell you –
when – whee! straight up to the ceiling.
I ask you.
I almost stuck there but
a neat side-flip
on the way down,
a clever little wheelie and I
was rolling down the road –
a free pancake!
Then I slipped up,
trying to show off,
and it was a case of
out of the frying pan
and into a pig's mouth!
Well, I ask you –
which would you rather be
swallowed by a pig
or a person?

Kite

Anon

A kite on the ground
is just paper and string
but up in the air
it will dance and will sing.
A kite in the air
will dance and will caper
but back on the ground
is just string and paper.

On Windy Days

Daphne Lister

On windy days we take our kites,
Unwind the strong, thin strings,
And soon the sky is full of shapes
Of floating, coloured wings.

As paper birds and butterflies,
Orange and gold and red,
Fly in the air until the wind
Decides to go to bed.

Conkers

Clive Sansom

When chestnuts are hanging
Above the school yard,
They are little green sea-mines
Spiky and hard.

But when they fall bursting
And all the boys race,
Each shines like a jewel
In a satin case.

A Rhyme for a Nosey-Parker

Anon

Ask no questions
And you'll be told no lies;
Shut your mouth
And you'll catch no flies.

From What Shall I do?

Brian Lee

My finger squeaks in the steam on the pane –
    A house, a face, a boat.
One sweep of my sleeve and they are gone;
My vest and socks drip onto the lawn,
    There's no one about.
Don't want to stay in, or go out.
      What shall I do now, Mummy?
      What shall I do now?

Books, comics, and marbles, my clockwork train,
    Puzzles I've done before,
Cards and dominoes, a pistol and plane,
Tin soldiers, cars, a meccano crane
    All over the floor:
There's nothing to play with there.
      What shall I do now, Mummy?
      What shall I do?

A Rhyme for a Cry-Baby

Anon

Cry, baby, cry,
Punch him in the eye;
Hang him on a lamp-post
and leave him there to dry.

Pirate

Samuel Menashe

Like a cliff
My brow hangs over
The cave of my eyes
My nose is the prow of a ship

I plunder the world.

School Dinners

Anon

If you stay to school dinners
Better throw them aside;
A lot of kids didn't,
A lot of kids died.
The meat is made of iron,
The spuds are made of steel;
If that don't get you
The afters will.

Build a Bonfire

Anon

Build a bonfire, build a bonfire,
Put the teachers on the top;
Put the prefects in the middle,
And we'll burn the blooming lot.

When you get married

Anon

When you get married,
And your husband gets cross,
Just pick up the broom
And ask who's boss.

Woodchuck

Anon

How much wood would a wood-chuck chuck
If a wood-chuck could chuck wood?
He would chuck as much wood as a wood-chuck would
If a wood-chuck could chuck wood.

Choosing Shoes

Ffrida Wolfe

New shoes, new shoes,
Red and pink and blue shoes,
Tell me what would YOU choose
If they'd let us buy?

Buckle shoes, bow shoes,
Pretty pointy-toe shoes,
Strappy, cappy low shoes;
Let's have some to try.

Bright shoes, white shoes,
Dandy dance-by-night shoes,
Perhaps-a-little-tight shoes;
Like some? So would I.
BUT
Flat shoes, fat shoes,
Stump-along-like-that-shoes,
Wipe-them-on-the-mat shoes
O that's the sort they'll buy.

Big Sister, Young Brother

Janet A Smith

I've got a big sister,
Her name is Jane,
She's twenty feet high
And ever so plain,
With poking, pink fingers
And nasty brown curls.
What's the use of
Horrible girls?

I've got a young brother
His name is Bertie.
He's thin as a rail,
And ever so dirty.
With fighting and thumping
And nuisance and noise,
What's the use of
Horrible boys?

Careful Katie

Anon

Careful Katie cooked a crisp and crinkly cabbage;
Did careful Katie cook a crisp and crinkly cabbage?
If careful Katie cooked a crisp and crinkly cabbage,
Where's the crisp and crinkly cabbage careful Katie cooked?

Johnnie Crack and Flossie Snail

Dylan Thomas

Johnnie Crack and Flossie Snail
Kept their baby in a milking pail
Flossie Snail and Johnnie Crack
One would pull it out and one would put it back.

O it's my turn now said Flossie Snail
To take the baby from the milking pail
And it's my turn now said Johnnie Crack
To smack it on the head and put it back.

Johnnie Crack and Flossie Snail
Kept their baby in a milking pail
One would put it back and one would pull it out
And all it had to drink was ale and stout
For Johnnie Crack and Flossie Snail
Always used to say that stout and ale
Was *good* for a baby in a milking pail.

A Rhyme for a Stare-Cat

Anon

Stare, stare, like a bear,
Call your mother, "Ginger hair,"
Chase your father round a chair,
Like a sausage in the air.

A Rhyme for a Sneak

Anon

Tell tale tit,
Your tongue shall be slit
And all the dogs in this town
Shall have a little bit.

Betty Botter

Anon

Betty Botter bought some butter,
But, she said, this butter's bitter;
If I put it in my batter
It will make my batter bitter,
But a bit of better butter
Will make my batter better.
So she bought a bit of butter
Better than her bitter butter
And she put it in her batter
And it made her batter better,
So 'twas better Betty Botter
Bought a bit of better butter.

Our Street

L T Baynton

Our street is not a posh place,
Say the mums in curlers, dads in braces, kids in nothing.
Our street is not a quiet place.
Says our football match, our honking bikes, our shouts,
Our street is not a tidy place,
Say the lolly wrapper, chippie bags, and written-on walls.
Our street is not a lazy place,
Say the car washing dads, clothes washing mums, and
            marbling boys.
Our street is not a new place
Say the paint-peeled doors, pavements worn, and crumbly
            walls.
Our street is not a green place
Say the pavements grey, forgotten gardens, lines of cars.
But our street is the best
Says me.

Little Johnny's Confession

Brian Patten

This morning
    being rather young and foolish
    I borrowed a machine gun my father
    had left hidden since the war, went out,
    and eliminated a number of small enemies.
    Since then I have not returned home.

This morning
    swarms of police with tracker dogs
    wander about the city
    with my description printed
    on their minds, asking:
    "Have you seen him,
    He is seven years old,
    likes Pluto, Mighty Mouse
    and Biffo the Bear,
    have you seen him, anywhere?"

This morning
    sitting alone in a strange playground,
    muttering Youve blundered Youve blundered
    over and over to myself
    I work out my next move
    but cannot move;
    the tracker dogs will sniff me out,
    they have my lollypops.

A Busy Day

Michael Rosen

Pop in
pop out
pop over the road
pop out for a walk
pop in for a talk
pop down to the shop
can't stop
got to pop

got to pop?

pop where?
pop what?

well
I've got to
pop round
pop up
pop into town
pop out and see
pop in for tea
pop down to the shop
can't stop
got to pop

got to pop?

pop where?
pop what?